Is Grief a Women's Room?

Is Grief a Women's Room?

Some feminist aspects of practical theology in
responding to the death of a life partner

Revd V. Lee (Minister)
Dr. R. Eke (UWE Associate Lecturer)

ISBN: 1547041145
ISBN 13: 9781547041145

Dr. Richard Eke – Cert.Ed., B.Ed., M.A. (Ed)., Ph.D. He started an unsuccessful career in banking and insurance, becoming a teacher in West London, near Wormwood Scrubs prison. He then went on to be in the advisory service of ILEA. He served on the independent broadcasting authority on their primary education panel. He was a deputy Head and Head and then became Deputy Warden of a teachers' centre, before moving to Bristol where he joined the staff of what is now UWE. Before stepping down to the role of Associate Lecturer, he was Associate Dean in Education and the joint head of academic development in the Faculty of Humanities. He has sustained experience of analysing talk, including work at doctoral level. He has co-authored a book, edited a book and published several papers on R.E. including the British Journal of R.E.

Revd Veronica Lee – Cert.Ed., B.A., M.Ed., Dip.H.E. (Christian Ministry and Mission). She started her teaching career in the East End of London, before moving to Bristol. She was a Deputy Head in Bristol and a Head in Gloucestershire. She went on to become an Associate Lecturer at UWE, whilst training for the Ministry. She works in a local parish and was a full-time chaplain in the hospital. She has co-authored a chapter in a book, written a chapter for a book on Special Needs, taken part in a Schools' Council Project on Investigating Talk with Harold Rosen, and has a wide experience of the needs of bereaved people as well as direct personal experience.

Acknowledgements

T HE AUTHORS WOULD like to thank all the interviewees who so willingly participated in this study; for being so open and honest under such difficult circumstances.

This book is dedicated to the memory of John.

FOREWORD

THE DEATH OF a loved one, either a life partner or spouse, is, say Holmes and Rahe (1967), who developed their Life Stress Inventory, the most stressful event experienced in a person's life.

Since their pioneering work, Anglican theology has undergone a gradual evolution. Anglican ministers are often an early port of call for bereaved families seeking help with funeral arrangements and a dignified farewell to one of their loved ones. When we use the description Anglican, we hope readers will find that we are mindful of the other churches in the Anglican communion, especially America's Episcopalian churches. Anglican responses vary and in this book, we explore some of these variations from the point of view of the bereaved. This perspective suggests that women play a significant role in such work. The authors argue that there is a long history to women's practical compassion towards the bereaved. Following a detailed and transparent analysis of seven interviews with those who have experienced the death of a loved one, the authors recommend that Anglican priests, whether men or women, might see the support and care of the bereaved as parish team work. In so doing, the authors draw on strands of practical theology and feminist theology. In reflecting on the significance of their work for the initial and in-service of ordinands, they offer narratives for reflection and some recommendations for reflective practice, including a critical response to the well-known account provided by Kubler-Ross.

CONTENTS

INTRODUCTION

THIS BOOK SETS out to explore ways in which bereavement support, for bereaved spouses can be enhanced. We have focused on bereaved spouses because there is evidence that the loss of a spouse is a number one source of stress in contemporary life. Many researchers draw on the pioneering work of Holmes and Rahe (1967) in their development of a Social Readjustment Rating Scale. This scale was designed as a predictor of the onset of serious illness although its subsequent validation and wider application makes it relevant to our study. In particular, they identified, working with 5,000 medical patients, that the death of a life partner is the number one stress factor, often a precursor to illness. It also has social consequences that can be both cultural and at the same time very personal. This is true of other forms of bereavement and while we have not visited these areas, we hope that our work may be applicable more widely. Our initial soundings led us to begin our explorations with a focus on the role of women in supporting the bereaved. We shall do this using both historical (Chapters 3 and 4) and contemporary sources (Chapters 2, and 5 to 14).

The 21st century has seen a growth of potential carers for those who are bereaved, although it is often those in the medical profession, who care for the dying, with whom the bereaved first share their pain. However, there are outside agencies, for example, hospice care, and the Macmillan and Marie Curie nurses who have a particular role in offering care for both the dying and the bereaved. Western cultures also offer the support of workers meeting the bereaved in a psychotherapeutic capacity.

If we are to be accurate we would need to confess to a particularly narrow set of interests. Our focus is narrow because it is on the work of what might be thought of as a particularly English group, namely, ordained and lay ministers of the Anglican church working in England. It is also narrow in the sense that we focus on the work of Anglican ministers in offering pastoral care to the recently bereaved. Although our focus is narrow, we believe the audience for our work might be wider. We think the narratives that have been shared with us by bereaved spouses will offer insights to ordinands in training, ministers and experienced priests and other committed Christians of the Anglican church, of the Episcopalian church and of related faith traditions. This by no means exclusive list can be extended to those with experience of working with the bereaved as well as those whose family members have recently lost a life-partner.

We shall be exploring ways in which death and mourning have been dealt with in the past and ways in which it is currently positioned and managed by the bereaved, and their pastoral support. We will not seek to generalise and, despite its title, will seek to engage with all those involved in bereavement and related pastoral care. We hope that through our initial focus on the Biblical, and especially Biblical womanhood, we will show the genesis of an acknowledgement of the gifts that strong women bring to their faith. Alongside this, we shall refine our focus to the role of women in sustaining the bereaved. We shall acknowledge the importance and value of the Judaic tradition as well as tracing fragments of the voice of women through the Middle Ages and beyond. These sources provide footings on which we shall build our material as well as contrasts that throw into relief the uniqueness of the role of women in contemporary Christian responses to bereavement and the bereaved. Looking at what we can learn from women working in the Christian tradition, need not exclude men, but can be seen as opening a door to wider pastoral possibilities

Most deaths occur either in hospital (Department of Health 2008), accessed on 09.09.2016) a hospice, or at home. However, there are exceptions to this where there is a sudden death for example, the accident, the suicide, the murder or in the line of duty. For the bereaved the death of a loved one who is extremely poorly, and is in a hospital, hospice or at home is generally an expected death, but even anticipated deaths come as a shock to the bereaved. (It is not our intention at this time, to consider bereavement as a result of assisted dying.) However, a sudden death, even as a consequence of treatment, can shake the very foundations of a bereaved person's life. The experience of the bereaved person, therefore, is as unique as the death of their loved one.

Their grief is likely to be a deeply personal experience and at the same time it becomes a special kind of social experience during which the bereaved are likely to re-visit their sense of self and their social identity. We are seeking to assert and reflect upon who reaches out to those who care for the bereaved and to understand the special contribution that women can bring to this process. We will try to achieve this by engaging with the narratives of some bereaved persons. We shall listen to their stories respectfully and try to hold on to their uniqueness as we re-tell them here in this book. In our re-tellings we will try and give voice to the ways in which our narrators re-cast their experiences of bereavement and those whom they see as significant in making meanings about the death of their loved one.

We are going to use a very small sample to show the importance of honouring the distinctiveness of their accounts of bereavement and the changes these wrought in their lives. Our informants will be from those actively in a church setting and those who are not. We will then seek to suggest ways in which people's gifts for caring for the bereaved can be used constructively, perhaps even transforming current trends and beliefs about the ways in which the bereaved grieve and how they should be supported. We intend to problematise assertions such as: 'time heals' and 'life goes on'. Amongst the themes we intend to explore, we shall ask: 'does time really heal? and 'in what ways does life go on?'

There are several significant writers on the themes of death and bereavement and particularly well known are the works of Kubler-Ross (1969) and the Stroebes(1999) who made great advances in both talking about and describing the processes of grief, and these provide a yardstick to which we will relate our narrators' stories of bereavement. We will suggest, from our data, that grief is not a steady state, but varies daily. Our interviewees all talked about the ways in which they coped with grief which were "the same" yet "not the same". It is our view that this has implications for those who work with the bereaved, train others to work with the bereaved, and offer on-line support for all of them.

In our research, we interviewed seven people who were willing to share their stories and experiences and although it was a limited number of people, nevertheless their insights will help us re-cast earlier accounts of grieving. We are mindful that it has been claimed that studies of bereavement and grief are inclined to make large claims on the basis of small data sets. However, a case can be made that seven interviewees are sufficient for the purposes of this study. While it can be argued (Baker S.E.& Edwards R. 2012 accessed 09.10,2015) that the number of interviews necessary for any project will vary with the nature and scope of the project itself, we are following the position adopted by Guest et al (2006) that saturation (no new material arises) occurs within the first twelve interviews. Guest et al also note that no new underpinning themes reflecting taken for granted social underpinnings (metathemes) arise after six interviews. Since it is our intention to explore the limits of existing constructions of bereavement and grief and point towards new ways of conceptualising the way assistance might be proffered by Anglican ministers, we consider seven interviews reflects the scale of our exploration.

We hope our readers will find a respect for more than one faith tradition; although we will exercise a particular focus on Christianity and especially the Anglican traditions. This is transcending the boundaries sometimes marked out by believers. The boundaries are not necessarily intentional, because they spring from one caring for another (Nodding 2003) who may draw on their faith and unknowingly create boundaries between themselves and the ones cared for: this perspective is about holding faith and respecting the dignity of the bereaved and the social and personal processes of grieving.

Our engagement with grief, grieving and bereavement has led us to understand that there needs to be respect for the bereaved, which involves caring, supporting and "being there" for them whilst they grieve. We want to understand the qualities of those who can walk alongside the bereaved, accompanying them with respectful affection. This might be the 'rumour of angels,' intimated by Berger (1970).

Women are important in grief because grief is a social process that usually depends on women's capacities. It is women who deal with the practicalities of death – of making sure that the family are fed, that they are effective listeners, and consolers. In Judaic/Christian history, it would appear to have always been women who were primarily involved with grief and bereavement. We can see this in the lives of women in the Bible, for example the story of Ruth and Naomi, where Naomi, having suffered the deaths of both her sons and her husband, tried to persuade her two daughters-in-law to leave her and go back to Moab. However, Ruth refuses to leave her, saying:

> "Do not press me to leave you or to turn back from following you!
> Where you go, I will go; where you lodge, I will lodge; your people
> shall be my people and your God my God. Where you die, I will
> die - there will I be buried….."
>
> (Ruth 1:16-17 NRSV 1995)

Throughout history, the caring of the dying has principally been the remit of women (Cheris Kramarae & Dale Spender 2000:300). In Medieval Europe the washing and laying out of the dead and preparing them for burial has been performed by women with experience who would also organise the mourning both before and after the funeral (Margaret Schaused 2006:194) And of course these observances became much further reaching in the Victorian era. (1837-1901).

The role of women in extending compassion to the bereaved, especially in the Anglican tradition, is one theme of our work. A second theme is to visit the specific pain that the death of a life-partner brings to the bereaved, and a third theme is an inclusive conception of the Anglican church. We shall explore these themes by looking at some of the historical antecedents of the current position of Anglican women in grief and then look at contemporary narratives about the loss of a loved one. We are thus using the historical to pave our way to the contemporary and in so doing we hope to use the former to highlight aspects of the latter.

1

TALKING ABOUT GRIEF

I N 1806, REVD. William Holland wrote in his diary:

> "Chatted with Mr. Northey as I rode home and had a Funeral. Old
> Kibby was 83 and yet his sister cried and seemed half distressed. I
> could not forbear observing that she could not expect him to live for
> ever, and therefore she might moderate her grief....."
>
> (Ayres. Ed. 2003:131)

It is unlikely that any Anglican would express their thoughts in so direct a
fashion. In modern parlance it might be:

> "I haven't done many of these visits before..... I'm not quite sure how
> to go about them"

It is as if there was a tradition of dismissing the grief of others that runs
through the generations, albeit that the disposal of grief is an experience that
seems easily managed. We want to explore this perception here.

In opposition to the thread of almost ignorance of the role of the
clergy in sustaining the bereaved, in understanding grief we understand a
process, (Kubler-Ross 1969) and the process is one of faith, (Ewan Kelly

2008) of individual, personal transformation from being a part of someone else to a person standing on their own. It is this standing alone that is ironically intrinsically social. We see three strands to grief, namely, faith, personal and then social: three strands plaited together in the experience of grief.

If we unpick the plait, then sometimes the weaving of faith is only from the one caring for the bereaved – the one cared for might be an agnostic or an atheist, so the special role of faith may be reified – faith doesn't exist separately from those who hold it dearly. For the believer, Jesus is a real presence in their ministry to the bereaved. Within a faith tradition grief is not separate from the griever and his/her feelings about the deceased. The believer is naturally more concerned for the bereaved as their faith assures them of the salvation of the deceased. It is part of the continuing process of the divine essence. It brings confidence about the deceased whether or not the deceased had a strong belief or not. For those who grieve that belief can be a comfort.

Faith guides the one ministering and can guide the one bereaved in dealing with the overwhelming sense of loss. Faith brings hope and comfort to those sustaining the bereaved. That hope enables those caring for the bereaved to listen to them with compassion and kindness.

Sometimes because bereavement and grief are inextricably bound up with one another, there is a thought that we can categorise different kinds of bereavement and think that we can diagnose and treat different kinds of grief. However, not only is grieving a social process, but we recognise, as Julian Barnes reminds us: "One grief throws no light upon another" (2013:70) Grief, therefore, is very personal. While conversations about another's grief can be analysed, grief itself cannot be dissected: one instance of grief cannot be understood to stand for others. We intend to learn through listening to narratives about the uniqueness of grief and the ways in which people respond.

We mean to engage in new territories of grief which depart from both the substance and the methodology of Kubler-Ross (1969). Her work, albeit it about the dying, has for many years served as a beacon for those committed to supporting the bereaved. In fact, she wrote the book partly to expose and partly to provoke the poor training doctors received in dealing with dying patients and their families. The book's transformative model of grief was subsequently described as 'literally rocking the medical profession" with a resultant public outcry for compassionate care. (Schillace 2015:147). It might also have been taken as a beacon for priests in their engagements with the dying and with the grieving. Although Kubler-Ross' book was essentially concerned with the dying, it was rapidly transformed into a concern for the grieving. The commonalities that she sees are given to the bereaved as a kind of guidebook with key stages clearly identified. Bereavement begins with denial, numbness, shock and isolation which act as a defence mechanism. There can also be a stage of bargaining whereby prior to the death, the bereaved can have 'promised' to do something in order to 'save' a dying person's life. This can lead to anger whereby the bereaved can be angry with themselves as well as angry with the person who has died and whoever (be it God or not) that they have bargained with. Sometimes those closest to the bereaved can detach themselves and be non-judgemental when they experience the anger of someone who is very upset. There is also the stage of guilt, whereby the bereaved may worry about whether they could have done something to help the dying person. Sometimes acute anxiety and anger can lead to the bereaved becoming depressed. The 'final' stage of grief is acceptance. There is an assumption that once 'acceptance' is reached that the bereaved are able to carry on as before and face the world as before with 'objectivity and detachment'. This approach has been valued because it is linear and easy to measure. It also offers the promise of a conclusion to grief.

The template that she developed from her analysis of the support for the dying filled a gap as it offered guidance for supporting the bereaved. The problem with this is that the template and its compassionate application became a mould into which the grief of the many was squeezed. The first problem here is that compassion for the dying is not synonymous with compassion for the bereaved. The second problem with this is that it denies the individuality of grief. It implies there is a general pattern which explains the passage of feeling for all grieving souls. We begin with an hypothesis that there is a difference in bereavement both in the death that precedes it and the unique sensitivities of those who are grieving. In this work, we shall acknowledge differences as much as similarities.

In transposing her conceptual framework for the dying into one for grieving, Kubler-Ross also enabled structure to be imposed where two world wars, continual global conflict and a diminishing influence for western religions had left a vacuum. We want to approach grief slightly differently and to acknowledge the pain, stress and dealing with being alone that the bereaved tell us about. Hereto we are seeking to cherish, savour and hold the chaos that the death of a loved partner brings.

In our research we shall acknowledge the trail-blazing work of Kubler-Ross, which has clearly been of value to those seeking to support the bereaved. In countless places we have found references to her work as if it sets out the steps that western grief will always follow. Others have acknowledged and moved beyond her innovative research, but for us, while appreciating her contribution, we also appreciate the individuality of grief and the dangers of attempting to impose order where there is little evidence for it and much to contradict it. Similarly, the Jewish Women's Network (accessed 02.01.2012) "were in agreement that in reality emotions don't come in neat packages." Perhaps the pattern of grief established in Kubler-Ross' work reflects her methodology. When employing survey data to study personal or community issues it is often easier to detect common patterns rather than unique expressions. We begin our research with caution and a particular reservation that there is no universal pathology of grief and thus we are likely to be concerned with differences alongside similarities.

Possibly a more realistic model of grief is that of the Stroebes (1999). They proposed the Dual Process Model of coping with bereavement, whereby they describe bereavement as swinging between loss and restoration. For example, the restoration of the bereaved person's life may be about getting on with life – such as going back to work, but just as they are 'getting on' with life, grief intrudes which sets the bereaved back – it could be a memory, a photo or even a piece of music. They subsequently describe their work as combining qualitative information with quantitative results. "We look beyond psychological information to sociological; epidemiological; medical; increasingly neuro-biological; physio-biological.....using these to derive hypotheses and guide our thinking." (personal communication 17.05.2015) Murray C.(2003 accessed 24.05.2015) in her "Grief, loss and bereavement" describes the characteristics of grieving as a set of 'unsteady, twisting and turning paths which require adaptation and change but have no specific end in sight.' This reflects a movement between coping with loss and moving forward, but it differs for each individual. These writers, taken together, offer powerful steers towards our methodology. We recognise that it is appropriate for us to draw on a wide range of sources to inform our thinking whilst, at the same time, we acknowledge the need to resist a grand meta-narrative of grief and grieving.

As Julian Barnes (2013:107) says:

"Four years on, some say to me, 'You look happier – making the advance on better' The bolder then add, 'Have you found someone?' As if that were obviously and necessarily the solution. For some outsiders it is; for others not. Some kindly want to 'solve' you, others remain attached to that couple which no longer exists and for them finding someone would be almost offensive."

Even after four years, Barnes was still coming to terms with being alone, yet was conscious that he did not quite 'fit' into society. People were anxious to 'normalise' him, which aligned him well with, for example, Kubler-Ross. Barnes is familiar with ideas of a completed period of grieving. He illustrates satisfactory conclusions.

Perhaps the most 'externally satisfying' outcome is restitution of the 'couple' status. Our observations point to this being particularly prevalent amongst bereaved men. It is interesting to note that after a few years, it is the widows who become far more adjusted to their single state than widowers who 'contemplated marriage quite soon after bereavement' (Jalland 1999:251). From our experiences, and from talking with widows, widows tend to seek the company of other women with whom they feel 'safe' – as one widow put it:

> "I know I don't have to put on a pretence. I can be 'me' – if I want to cry or to talk about my husband, I know they (women) will listen to me. If I talk to a man in the same way, be becomes embarrassed, so I shut up."
>
> (conversation with a recent widow 2012)

Similarly, on talking about death, one female colleague said:

> "I wouldn't want to marry again. I've knitted one pattern, I don't want to have to knit another!"

She did not want to have to knit in another loving partner, which is hard work, and a serious business, knowing that it would have to be a very different pattern.

Writing for an edition of The Guardian (03.05.14 Family section) Ben Brooks-Dutton says:

> "I didn't just lose my wife, I lost my identity. I was ambitious and hardworking and Des (his wife) was too. We were always planning. We were going to have another child and were working towards buying a house. I was happy – then all of a sudden I'm not happy......
> everything I was about – my humour, everything – has changed. It's like I have no real idea of what I am or what my plan is for the

future,…..I don't really care, I used to be so focused and now maybe the focus is that I have no focus."

Here is a prime example of a widower's identity being that of a 'couple' which has suddenly been taken away from him, resulting in him oscillating between coping with everyday life and grief.

His sense that nobody can know anyone else's grief is expressed when he says:

"…the second year is said to be the hardest. Is it? It's different. But then grief is different. It's not like how I imagined. It's not how anyone imagines……"

(Guardian Family 03.05.2014)

The struggle that one individual has in understanding another person's grief and that one individual's grief is not necessarily mirrored in another's, implies that it is more or less impossible to take diverse accounts of grief and classify them. This leads us to question the solidity of Kubler-Ross' analysis.

Perhaps one of the most strident critiques of classificatory work of this kind is found in post-modern feminism. (Fraser N. & Nicholson L. 1988). They argue that research might better acknowledge differences rather than searching for similarities. This is a premise that we shall carry through to our interview analysis.

The sense of loss associated with the death of a life partner never goes away. It gives rise to a deeply personal grief that might intertwine this sense of loss with a changing sense of self. When those bereaved in this way begin to talk about their grief, we can recognise that uniqueness, but we can also see some possible commonalities in shared and social aspects of grieving.

One example of this dates from the late 1970's where Roche (1979:69) reports on how many widows constantly refer to the support and understanding of other women:

"It was the girls at work who saw me through.."

Roche (1979:69) also makes reference to a welfare officer who visited the widow every day during the last weeks of her husband's illness and for some weeks after the funeral. It was this sort of behaviour that resonated most with the widows in the report. Their understanding of support was not only about people coming to visit them, but also of still being accepted as the same person they were before their spouse's death. The widows were aware they would need to make adjustments to their lives, but felt that they were able to do this more effectively with good support.

Interestingly Ben Brooks-Dutton goes on to comment:

"It's easy for everyone to become your counsellor or vice versa and sometimes quite selfishly, 'I can't be this for you today' and that in itself leaves you feeling like crap."

(Guardian Family 03.05.2014)

He continues by saying:

"All of a sudden this memory of Desreen – nothing that would mean anything to anyone – popped into my head and I felt myself laugh."

(Guardian Family 03.05.2014)

Ben is aware that there is a grief dialogue in which others try and engage him, but there are days when he is unable to engage with this, which makes him feel awful. Yet there are other times when he is able to laugh at his fond recollections. Neither the narratives we have collected nor those in the public domain point to any consistent pattern in individuals' responses to the loss of a loved partner.

As Schillace (2015:36-39) reminds us "the problem lies in the concept of normal......when medical authorities tell us that two weeks or two months is sufficient, it creates a cultural expectation that grieving is firstly a short process with recognisable steps and secondly something that we must get over in order to return to normal.." She goes on to say: "those of us who have grieved know better...(as we shall see). In Victorian England, the stages of grief were specific and lengthy; a year was not too long for mourning a husband..." Following Schillace we would suggest that neither two months nor a year are 'normal' – both assumptions are equally flawed.

Schillace's (2015:36-39) guidance that those of us who have grieved know better finds echoes in Lyttle's (2002) study. He recommends that 'theoretical concepts of grief should be integrated with experiential data and narrative methods.' Despite a possibly mandatory, probably inappropriate care quality framework, that Lyttle attaches to provision for the bereaved, this is nonetheless a very useful suggestion that aligns well with the work reported here and the direction in which it takes us.

Following Stroebe M. (personal e-mail 17.05.2015) we consider it helpful to think about contemporary explanations of grief: what is in effect a neuroanatomy (Gundel et al 2003) of grief. Researchers have recently sought a kind of demonstration of psychiatric truths through appealing to contiguous biological events. It has to be acknowledged that writers tend to avoid simplistic causes or explanations. Hanson (2007) for example, suggests that grief has many psychological elements and thus draws on many resources of the brain, including those dealing with attention, memory, emotion, planning, language, relationships and, in particular we would suggest, attachment. So, Hanson (2007) says: "the experience of grief tends to activate both specific brain areas linked to the aspect of grief that is primary in the moment, and the more general network of structures and processes."

By 2012, Everly and Lating were arguing that grief is mercurial, again demonstrating our supposition that there is no universal pathology of grief and hence we need to be cautious when dealing with the almost deterministic accounts of grief offered by neuro-science.

In this chapter, we have drawn on some contemporary sources of grief including Jalland 1999, Barnes 2013, Brooks-Dutton 2014 and Schillace 2015. We have also made reference to some more "technical" explorations of grief including Kubler-Ross 1969 and the Stroebes 1999. We have tried to stitch these together to present a perspective of grief at the loss of a life partner which resists a grand narrative of grief in which one loss can be said to reflect on another: rather we have hypothesised the uniqueness of the circumstances relating to every individual death and a comparable uniqueness in every individual's grief.

2

THE WAYS IN WHICH JEWISH PEOPLE DEAL WITH DEATH AND MOURNING

I N 1994, THE Jewish Women's Network (JWN accessed 02.01.2012) published a booklet entitled "Bereavement Booklet for Jewish Women." This was in response to the ways in which women could be moved forward with regard to their involvement in funerals and bereavement, since 'historically it had been the province of men in the Jewish community to actively arrange and participate in bereavement rituals." The Network repeatedly asked themselves whether they were "including all women across the spectrum." This was especially so when we consulted on the customs and practices of different sections of the community and we were frequently told 'it depends on who you ask.'" Nonetheless, some communities may continue to see women's desire to say Kaddish as providing "a threat to existing male status in the community." (JWN accessed 02.01 2012), Lamm (2000) acknowledges that there has been considerable movement on the issue of women reciting Kaddish,

> "Today, virtually all synagogues follow the Sephardic custom that all mourners in the synagogue recite Kaddish simultaneously and do so while standing at their own seats, no matter in which section of the synagogue
>
> (Lamm 2000:161)

On a cold February day in New Jersey, we sat in a Rabbi's office in a synagogue sharing lunch together. My American friend had introduced us so that we could talk about the ways in which Jewish people deal with death and mourning. The Rabbi was still in mourning for her parent.

We talked about bereavement and that often dying has become so medicalised that it has left people without any experience in mourning and bereavement, leaving many people uncomfortable with bereavement as a result. The medicalisation of dying has been accompanied by the medicalisation of grief. Some American medical authorities (Schillace 2015:35) allow grief to continue for two months, after which it becomes depression and therefore treatable by medical professionals. The Rabbi, still mourning months after the death of her parent, was behaving in a proper and appropriate manner in accordance with her faith. She was supported in this by her family and by her religious community who understood that grieving takes more than a couple of months to come to terms with.

The Rabbi went on to talk about Jewish rituals connected with death and also about the history attached to these. She told me of how Abraham bought a grave for Sarah, his wife – hence the connection with burials and Judaism – this buying of a grave, in Hebron, became a symbol of eulogising and crying for her. Jacob's wife, Rachel is buried in a grave in Ephrat, where Jacob set up a pillar on her grave so that she could be remembered (Gen.35:16-21 NRSV 1995). It is important, therefore, for Jewish people to buy a grave prior to their death. Learning from this, we can recognise that in the midst of our lives there are our deaths and we should be prepared. Or as Schillace (2015:66) says: "Life and death exist always together, like summer and winter.."

The Rabbi also talked about 'shivah' – Maurice Lamm in "The Jewish Way in Death and Mourning" (2000:132) says that:

"The fundamental purpose of the condolence call during *shivah* is to relieve the mourner of the intolerable burden of intense loneliness."

Lamm (2000:132-141) goes on to say that this is a time when the bereaved person withdraws from society and has time to grieve. The mourner's house is open from the time people come from the graveside (Jewish people are traditionally buried within 24 hours of death), until seven days later – day one being the day of the burial. The front door is left open and people visiting the bereaved do not speak until the mourner talks; the visitor sits and listens. They will speak about the deceased and often tell special stories about them. The visitor will bring food, as the mourner is not allowed to make food. As the Jewish Women's Network also says: "It is not helpful to offer advice about how the mourner should feel or respond to their loss." (JWN accessed 02.01,2012). There are restrictions on the mourner who is not allowed to work, bathe (however they do bath now), shave, or wear leather shoes. They are only allowed to leave the house to go to the synagogue. The bereaved is then left with the combination of focusing on their loss, but also becomes exhausted with the amount of visitors! However, not being left alone ensures the mourner has company and that they get fed – the first meal being of eggs (symbolising re-birth), lentils and bagels (something round which gives a message of comfort). The visitor will often give the bereaved a hug and then leave. In this way, the visitor does not come out with the wrong words. On leaving they will say: "May God comfort you among the other mourners of Zion and Jerusalem" (Lamm 2000:119)– thereby connecting the bereaved with others in the past who have been bereaved and reminding them that they are part of a community.

After the seventh day of Shivah, the mourner is permitted to leave the house and has to walk until they see a car (previously this was a horse and carriage) – they therefore walk until they see life is normal.

For Rabbis, this is a significant element of their faith tradition bearing profound commentary from scholars who extend their hand across history. Rabbis are expected to be aware of debates within their faith and the authenticity of the Rabbinical sources on which they draw. As a consequence of this, Rabbis, whether men or women, have a thorough grounding in appropriate ways of responding to bereaved members of their community.

Anglican funerals provide, for many, a beginning of grief processes. We shall suggest later in this book that funerals are but a beginning to processes of grieving, not an end. Firstly, it is entirely appropriate for a minister to visit or make contact with the bereaved as soon as they possibly can. They will also need to demonstrate a sensitivity in understanding if the bereaved would welcome visits from others. Early bereavement and funereal arrangements are not the end of the matter. Jewish traditions accept that grieving does not stop at the time of the funeral and may go on for months and indeed years. Some Anglican ministers may need to recognise when it is appropriate to continue to provide comfort to the bereaved and how such comfort can help the bereaved live with their grief and also live their lives to the full; they do not have such a strong scholarly tradition of response to grief to guide them in such matters. They should also be aware of significant anniversaries in the lives of their parishioners and carry that knowledge with sensitivity and compassion.

The Rabbi also told us that on the death of a spouse it is customary, in Jewish rituals, for the children to support the surviving parent by, for example, taking care of the things the deceased used to do in the house. In this way, they are filling in the gaps of the loss in practical ways. The children will also talk about the deceased parent and understand the legacy left by that person and therefore keep the legacy alive.

One thing an Anglican minister should not be afraid to do is to hold and perhaps cherish, something of the identity of the deceased. They should also be aware that they need to provide an opportunity for the bereaved to talk about and share stories about the deceased and not necessarily ones that provide information to take away in order to write the eulogy. This sharing has a breadth of time, acknowledging that grief is a long process. It is inclusive. It recognises the grief of family and friends and is open to their needs. The Jewish Women's Network Bereavement Booklet for Women (JWN accessed 02.01.2012) cites a bereaved person talking about her father's life:

"I may remember. I don't want to remember anything. I may notice. I don't want to notice anything. I will keep busy, a positive busy, something to do during the jerky fracture of my father's life…mind a memorial to him, a more lasting obituary than three lines in the expensive columns of the Jewish Chronicle. I will keep him alive. I will let him go."

This is a clear example of how grief affects people. Grief comes in 'waves'. Some days are more positive than others. Some days are like a black hole. Grief does not conform to any 'rules' or 'timetables'. It is something that never entirely goes away. It is always there, sometimes in the back of our minds, sometimes at the forefront.

As Judy Grahn (The Work of a Common Woman 1982 In J.W.N. accessed 02.01.2012)) says:

This is what is so odd
About your death:
That you will be 34 years old
The rest of my life.
We always said that we would be around we two in our old age
& I still believe that,
however when I am 80
you will still be 34,
& how can we ever understand
What each other has been through?

Kaddish, for parents, takes place for thirty days after death and, nowadays, is often said for close family members as well. The bereaved promise to contribute to charity so that the soul of the deceased may be 'bound in the Bond of Life'.

When High Holidays are imminent, many Jewish people visit cemeteries in order to pay their respects for their dead. Sometimes a Rabbi may recite the El Mal'e Rachamim, which is a Hebrew memorial prayer to God and which is in turn recited by the mourner. The prayer asks God to:

"Grant perfect rest beneath the sheltering wings of Your presence..."

(Lamm 2000:256)

It would appear that Christian people have come a long way from their Jewish roots in their understanding of mourning and condolence. There is an expectation that after the funeral (often taking place between one and two weeks after the death), the bereaved will start to resume their normal life. As the Reverend William Holland remarked of Old Kibby's sister they are expected to moderate their grief. People certainly visit, but often it is the women who visit as men find the emotional aspect of bereavement difficult to cope with, as will be seen from some of the dialogues with the people we interviewed.

There is a similarity as regards remembering the deceased, however, in the Service for All Souls which is held annually in some Christian churches. As we hope is apparent from our discussion of Jewish endowments to Anglican ministers, this Remembrance lasts for rather more than one day a year.

In this chapter, we have shared something of a conversation with an American Rabbi about Judaic mourning traditions. It is clear that these traditions require adherents to recognise that in the midst of their lives they should be prepared for death. There is also a recognition that grief extends beyond the two months that some medical practitioners believe sufficient. Interestingly, there are also some fairly clear rules for all mourners including men to follow. We have also suggested that beyond a eulogy, Anglican visitors might take a special role in acknowledging the life of the deceased. This might be extended to acknowledging the continuing wish of the bereaved to ask God for the deceased that He "grant perfect rest beneath the sheltering wings of your presence." (Lamm 2000:256)

3

REFLECTIONS ON WOMEN IN THE EARLY CHURCH AND GRIEF-RELATED TEXTS BY MEDIEVAL WOMEN

IN SEARCHING FOR a fuller understanding of how women care for the bereaved and their grief, we think it is pertinent to explore what has happened in the past. In this chapter we shall be offering brief cameos of the work of some Christian women from the emergence of the early church through to the late Middle Ages. In the subsequent chapter we shall move from "the age of Enlightenment" to the twenty first century. In this chapter, we are reflecting on the role of women in the early church and their subsequent derogation, and on the writings of Christian women in the early and later Middle Ages. We intend to begin to examine something of the unique ways, both practical and spiritual, in which women aided and comforted the bereaved.

The development of the early church has been thoroughly analysed with MacCulloch (2009) offering a recent and fulsome history. He seeks to give "due weight......to the tangled and often tragic relations between Christianity and its mother – monotheistic Judaism, as well as its monotheistic younger cousin, Islam." (2009:4)

If we go back in history, the Judaic/Christian people were taught that along with cattle and slaves, wives were the property of their husbands.

Women were expected to 'be anonymous in order to pass on the social norm'. (Grey 1993:39). In Ephesians for example, Christian wives were instructed to:

> Be subject to your husbands as you are to the Lord. For the husband is the head of the wife......
>
> (Ephesians 5:22-24 NRSV 1995)

Paul includes women as named recipients of all of his authenticated letters, as MacCulloch (2009) reminds us, he strangely excludes their presence at the Resurrection. Although there were women heads of church groups in Paul's time, such as Lydia, the purple-dyer, Phoebe, the deacon and Junia the apostle, Paul is still reluctant to trust or give responsibility to women. Paul writes:

> "Let a woman learn in silence and all submissiveness. I permit no woman to teach or have authority over men; she is to keep silent. For Adam was formed first and then Eve; and Adam was not deceived but the woman was deceived and became a transgressor."
>
> (1 Tim 2:11-15 NRSV 1995))

What we learn from this early material is both how capable women were in the early church and how uncomfortable their competence seemed to make men feel.

Luise Schotroff (in Grey 1993:33) goes on to say that 'later the Christian men said it more clearly. Eve slept with the snake and thereby brought sin into the world'. The only way in which women can atone for their 'sin' is through experiencing the pain of childbirth. As a result, both biblically and culturally, women were regarded as inferior to men. Men were, even two thousand years ago, being taught that they were the responsible ones, because it was Eve who succumbed to temptation first and was therefore responsible for sin coming into the world. Men are, as a result, the only capable ones of being the heads of households and the only ones with authority. John Calvin in Grey (1993:35) sums up Eve's guilt being passed down to all women by saying:

"God is better pleased with a woman who considers the conditions God has assigned her to as a calling, and submits to it, not refusing to bear the distaste of food, the illness, the difficulty or rather the fearful anguish associated with childbirth or anything else that is her duty....In the punishment itself are the means of securing salvation."

However, this seems to be in direct contrast with the stories of some of the women in the Old Testament. Esther, for example, by listening and watching and biding her time was able to save an entire nation. (NRSV1995 Esther 1-10) Rahab enabled the spies that Joshua sent, to return safely to him (NRSV1995 Joshua 2). These two illustrations suggest that God also favoured strong, confident, independent women. If we turn to the New Testament we can also find stories of 'Spirited Women' (2000: Ashcroft). The Samaritan Woman is depicted as a person who dares to argue with Christ – not only was she a non-Jew and as such an outsider, but she was also a woman. Christ has no difficulty in giving her insight into 'living water' (NRSV 1995: John 5:14-25)

At Christ's death, it is noticeable that his mother, his mother's sister - Mary, the wife of Clopas, Mary Magdalene and John were at the foot of the cross staying with him whilst he died, and grieving for him. When Christ was carried down from the cross, John's Gospel reports that Joseph of Arimathea and Nicodemus tended to him quickly and put him into a tomb. It would appear on reading this that Joseph and Nicodemus attended to the practicalities of burial, leaving the women to grieve. Luke's Gospel also reports on the (grieving) women who followed Christ, wanting to put spices and ointments on his body, but being unable to, due to the imminence of Passover, and had returned later on, only to find his body gone. John's Gospel also talks about Mary Magdalene finding the tomb empty, running to find the disciples, who on discovering Christ's body gone, went home. It was Mary, who remained weeping outside the tomb and is subsequently the first person to see Christ resurrected. (1995 NRSV John 19 and 20)

Here we see the capacity of women not only to share their grief but to share the Resurrection with both women and men. We see women as able to carry grief and able to communicate powerfully, arguably, Christianity's most important message. A good example of the subsequent invisibility of women in the church has been thoughtfully documented by Greer in "The Obstacle Race", Chapter VIII 'The Cloister' (Greer 1981:151ff) where she argues that convents "unless they enjoyed exceptional favour, came low down" (Greer: 1981:159).

Despite the early traditions of women's roles in bereavement and grief, women are particularly occluded during the dark ages. The first clear contribution to Christian documents by a woman appeared to be those preserved in Gerona Cathedral 970 (Greer 1981:152) There is a continuous thread of Christian women's writings following on this first illustrative work and we shall explore some of the themes relevant to grief, that are embodied in these texts. Powerful men were educated, whereas women were not, although those serving as abbesses and some middle-class nuns were probably literate. Towards the end of that period we find a celebration of the role of women in Christianity in Hildegard of Bingen's (1098-1179) delightful "Quia ergo femina"

Because a woman brought death
a bright Maiden overcame it,
and so the highest blessing
in all of creation
lies in the form of a woman,
since God has become man
in a sweet and blessed Virgin.

(H. de Bingen. trans. 2001:118)

Her compassion and scholarship were evident in her verse and in her actions. The verses we have cited reconfigure the religious positioning of women. Her actions included providing for example a Christian burial for a young man who had been excommunicated. She cited her reasons for so doing to be that he had repented and received the Sacrament of the Sick and Dying. Although her convent was subjected to an interdict for her doing this, her protestations resulted in this being revoked. (Kiefer:1999 accessed 17.10.2014)

Between the twelfth century and the fourteenth, there seems to be something of a gap. Writing in the fourteenth century, we see that a concern with compassion comparable to that of Hildegarde, infuses the work of Julian of Norwich. (c.1342-1416). Indeed, she prays for compassion alongside 'absolute contrition' and steadfast longing toward God' (Graves. D. accessed 17.10.2014)

Her visions were recorded, (c.1373) and we have a particular interest in her thirteenth vision where she received an answer to what is needed of her. Jesus' response is that it is necessary that there should be sin, but that

"All shall be well.
All shall be well
And all manner of thing shall be well"
(Julian of Norwich trans. By Graves D. n.d.)

It is a source of comfort both for those who are dying and also for the bereaved. This must have been exceptionally reassuring in a country and at a time when the population was ravaged by plague.

During the time of the Black Death, its impact on British society was such that over a quarter of the population died in the years 1348-1350 with six more occurrences until the end of the century. We speculate that for many, normal rituals were abandoned in part due to the numbers dying and in part due to the death of priests who were particularly vulnerable since they had to visit the sick to give the last rites. It is not surprising that some priests declined the opportunities to deliver the last rites at this time. Schillace (2015:79) talks of a 'restart' to death preparation.

In Medieval Europe, the washing and laying out of the dead and preparing them for burial had been performed by women with experience who would also organise the mourning, both before and after the funeral (Schaused M. 2006:194). Women, during the Black Death, must therefore, like priests, have been particularly vulnerable.

Christine de Pizan (1364-1430) argues vociferously against the subjugation of women:

"God similarly endowed women with speech, thank the Lord, for if He hadn't done so, they would all have remained dumb.......If women's speech had been as unreliable and worthless as some maintain, Our Lord Jesus Christ would never have allowed news of such a glorious miracle as his resurrection to be announced first by a woman, as he told the blessed Magdalene to do when he appeared to her first on Easter day and sent her to inform Peter and the other apostles."

(C. de Pizan:1999:27 trns)

Her woman of Reason goes on to say (C. de Pizan:1999:22 trns) that putting Adam to sleep and creating woman from one of his ribs was a sign that "she was meant to be his companion standing at his side whom he would love as if they were one flesh, and not his servant lying at his feet." This woman of Reason also felt that too many people presume that when God made man in his own image this implied his physical body and goes on to explain that it is not about the human form, but about the soul and the intellect, and that God:

"endowed both male and female with this soul, which He made equally noble and virtuous in the two sexes."

(C. de Pizan:1999:22-23 trns)

This forceful view of woman is in direct contrast to 1Timothy 2:11-15. (NRSV:1995). The strength of her views were such that she felt empowered to stand against conventional male tradition and extend compassion to those in need.

Christine de Pizan recounts stories of women's compassion, for example that of Nathalia who supported, comforted and stayed with her husband, Adrian, who was imprisoned as a consequence of his conversion, and also remained at his deathbed. She subsequently went to Constantinople where she played a special role in caring for the martyrs who had been killed and ensured their bodies were buried properly. (C. de Pizan: 1999:252-253 trns.)

Writing about a hundred years later, St. Teresa of Avila (1515-1582) finds similar cause for compassion from her meditations on Christ. The following quotation is attributed to her, which beckons the reader to remember that Christ's compassion works through each individual:

"Christ has no body now but yours. No hands, no feet on earth but yours. Yours are the eyes through which he looks with compassion on this world. Yours are the feet with which he walks to do good. Yours are the hands through which he blesses all the world. Yours are the hands, yours are the feet, yours are the eyes, you are his body. Christ has no body now on earth but yours."
(Teresa of Avila quotes accessed 17.10.2014)

We can note that significantly there was a belief that the prayers of women were the most effective. Abelard, in Paris, was recorded as "recommending a psalter to Heloise for prayers of the faithful, especially those of women on behalf of their dear ones and of wives for their menfolk" and making a specific request for religious women to pray as their prayers were felt to be the most effective (Schaused 2006:194). It seems extraordinary that women's prayers were felt to be more powerful than men's in a time when women were held in such low esteem.

Doubly significant then are the words and the actions of women who were powerful at the time. The few examples that we have offered for illustration, demonstrate a willingness to pray for others, compassion for both the dying and the bereaved, and a confidence that in this compassion they were realising their Christian selves.

Of course, medieval men were also reflecting on life, death and the bereaved. As Atkinson, cited in Paul K. (2015:213) remarks, the early church fathers were "decidedly disinterested in the subject of preparing to die." The text "The Art of Dying" (Ars Moriendi) filled that gap as Paul continues first with a longer text Tractatus artis bene moriendi – written by the Council of Constance (1414-1418) – and then with a shorter version Ars Moriendi published in 1450. As Paul notes the authors of these two texts are unknown, but were probably men. The longer 'tractatus' gives guidance to death bed supporters but the focus remains solidly on the dying (Paul: 2015:214). The shorter version concludes with "Everyman accepted into heaven with a host of angels" (2015:216). Jeremy Taylor, Anglican bishop writing for the Earl of Carbery, produced "Holy Dying" for the Earl's wife. As Paul tells us during the writing of this both Carbery and Taylor became widowers and the book, although an instruction manual, is written with "extraordinary tenderness and passion" (Paul:2015:216)

In this chapter, we have reflected on the compassionate role of women in bereavement beginning with the Crucifixion and its aftermath where women were at the foot of the Cross and at the tomb. As well as compassion we also find comfort, proper treatment of the dead, organising mourning and Christ's compassion working through people, communicated powerfully by words both spoken and written. We found written evidence of a continuing Christian tradition of women's reflection on their role and, indeed, on that of humanity in furthering God's will. This was accompanied by compassion and comfort in the lives and works of Hildegard of Bingen, Julian of Norwich, Christine de Pizan and St. Teresa of Avila. These remarkable women were the exception rather than the rule, although we have noted the compassion of ordinary women in the laying out of the dead and of praying for the deceased. We have acknowledged the important role that women played in death and dying. Whilst recognising that men were strategically placed in this process we have also acknowledged that it seemed to be women who undertook the basic responsibilities for caring for the dead and powerful religious women were amongst those who extended both comfort and prayers to the bereaved. All women seemed to have been involved in the practicalities of caring for the dead and the bereaved. Those who had the privilege of being scholarly women, were also involved in redefining and extending the contribution of women to their faith tradition.

We have alluded to the impact that the Black Death had on the rituals and rites surrounding death and the dying and the bereaved. Along with others we have suggested that this led to a reconfiguration of these rites and rituals. In some ways, the impact on both rituals and on women of this level of death across Europe prefigures the appalling death toll of two world wars and it is to this that our next chapter will lead.

Anglicans will recognise lessons here for the practice of their faith. Women from the time of Christ and throughout the Middle Ages, made a contribution to the faith tradition and particularly to the needs of the bereaved. Even in the constraining times of the Middle Ages, women were able to begin to redefine everybody's, and especially, women's work in the church. Their work in relation to grief and death were changed by circumstances. We shall go on to explore the lessons that might be taken from this period.

4

GRIEVING IN ENGLAND FROM THE LATER MEDIEVAL TO THE CONTEMPORARY

IN MEDIEVAL ENGLAND, everyday life was surrounded by death and dying. Life expectancy itself was pretty short by today's standards, averaging in the mid-forties. This was dependent upon surviving after the age of five, achieved by about two thirds of the population. The wealthier one was the longer one might expect to live and conversely life expectancy for the poorer (the majority) was shorter. This was dependent on them maintaining good health and avoiding death as a result of warfare. (Woodbury S. accessed 17.10.2014). For women, the challenge was to avoid death in childbirth since about 5% died in childbirth often with their baby and a further 15%, Woodbury tells us, died from puerperal fever.

We might observe in passing, that little has changed with regard to wealth and life expectancy. The Herald newspaper in Scotland (accessed 17.09.2016) reports that life expectancy for a Glaswegian male is 73 years while the male born in Hart in Hampshire could expect to live to 82.4 years, according to the Daily Mail's 50 Best Places to Live (accessed 17.09.2016)

As we have said in the previous chapter, in Medieval Europe the washing and laying out of the dead and preparing them for burial was performed by women with experience who would also organise the mourning both before and after the funeral. (Schaused M. 2006:194). Often it was the lowliest of women who laid out the dead, perhaps this offers some answer as to why women assumed the role of dealing with death and mourning. It should also be noted that during this period nurses who were in control of caring for the ill and terminally ill ended up tending to those who died. Again, it was the women who ultimately became 'responsible' for caring for the deceased. Women, in England, must have been seen as dealing better with the practicalities of death.

It has to be noted that in the times of the Black Death (1348-1350) bodies were not so carefully cared for. It became 'necessary' for people to be buried as quickly as possible, so the introduction of mass graves, where people were either buried in their own clothes or in some sort of shroud, became commonplace in order to stop the pestilence from spreading too quickly. It seems ironic that in this day and age, we have no better policy to apply to Ebola victims in West Africa.

In Tudor England, mourning reflected the social standing of the deceased and their family in both dress and observance of the rules of mourning. Women were expected to follow these rules with greater rigour than their male counterparts. As Ruiz (Ruiz Romero M.I. in her paper "The Ritual of the early modern death 1550-1650" (accessed 17.10.2014) notes "mourning was officially divided into phases – an intense period followed by an intermediate phase or phases and then normal behaviour could be resumed"

As regards tending the deceased, prior to burial these duties were likely to be performed by a member of the family. Towards the end of the Tudor epoch the coffin-maker was often called on and he used the services of local peasant women he knew to be available. They washed the body and then dressed it in a 'shirt', if male, or a 'shift' if female. On occasions, they would mask the smell of the decaying body using 'sprigs of sweet-smelling herbs'. (Ruiz Romero M.I. accessed 17.10.2014)

The Reformation was clearly established in England with reformer denominations appearing across Europe. As Schillace notes (2015:84) "the movement dampened certain celebrations that had been linked to Catholic traditions especially in terms of food and drink (and the impiety caused by all that inebriate conviviality)" Something of the symbolism associated with death has been expunged from English culture.

Preparations for the burial of the bodies of poorer members of the community would normally be conducted by the oldest female of the family 'who would wash and dress the body and lay it out on the best bed in the house while vigil was kept. Communal coffins were kept by most churches so that the deceased could be carried from home to the churchyard, after which the coffin was opened and the body taken out to be buried straight in the ground. If the family could afford it the minister would give a homily prior to burial and some generous parsons did so even for those who were unable to pay. (Regency Redingote accessed 17.10.2014)

It is also interesting to note that in the so-called 'Age of Enlightenment' some rather more ancient customs were still practised in England. For example, on the death of John Aubrey in1697, amongst his papers (Britten ed. 1881) were found a number of accounts of 'sinne-eating'. This practice may have derived from Hosea 4:8 "they feed on the sins of my people and relish their wickedness" (N.I.V. 1984). Aubrey tells us that in Shropshire, for instance, an elderly man would arrive at the house of the deceased, whereby he would be given payment (a groat), a stool facing the door, to sit on, a crust of bread to eat and a full bowl of ale to be downed in one. In other accounts (Aubrey in Britten 1881) a cake is eaten over the corpse. The sin-eater would then confirm that he had taken the sins of the departed upon his own soul. This act apparently allowed the deceased to rest in peace rather than having to 'walk' for evermore, and was still being practised in 1686.

Conceptualising the period from the late medieval to Georgian England, Houlbrooke (2000:376) suggests that five features characterise changing attitudes and practices in relation to death and grieving as follows:

New religious beliefs
Levels of mortality
Development of social structure
Spread of literacy
Rise of individualism

As Houlbrooke (2000:376) acknowledges in his discussion of this broad era the influence of these characteristics varied from 'one period to another'

Schillace (2015:87) tells us that by the dawn of the eighteenth century wooden coffins "with deep burials" had become more popular. At the same time monuments and markers similarly increased in popularity inscribed with appropriate prayers and images. Although by this time the majority did not, "technically", believe in intercession for or by the dead, she goes on to observe, (2015:88) "that England in particular struggled to put more spiritual death rituals into practice."

Houlbrooke (2000) discriminates between class and denomination and we can observe that he argues that the outward manifestations of grief, no matter how heartfelt, were increasingly disliked during the sixteenth and seventeenth centuries. The outward display of feelings had to be balanced with a sense of self-control.

The need for a sense of self-control is clearly articulated by Adam Smith in "The Theory of Moral Sentiments" (1759), perhaps his major work, eighteen years in the writing. This book is sadly less often cited than his somewhat lighter, ten years in the writing, "Wealth of Nations". In "The Theory of Moral Sentiments", he argues that since others will experience our grief, it is best restrained out of a respect for those others. In turn, he advocates that others should respect the mourner by being more sympathetic than would normally be expected of them:

> "He must flatten, if I may be allowed to say so, the sharpness of its natural tone, in order to reduce it to harmony and concord with the emotions of those who are about him. What they feel, will, indeed, always be, in some respects, different from what he feels, and compassion can never be exactly the same with original sorrow…"
>
> (Smith A. The Theory of Moral Sentiments
> 1759 page 4 accessed 17.10.2014)

By the end of the century medical attention to those who were dying came out of the shadows and the medical commitment to prolonging life began to replace the religious commitment for the care of the soul. (Schillace 2015)

The proper expressions of grief were better found in emotional graveyard poetry and similar romantic literature.

> "Slow through the church-way path we saw him borne,
> 'Approach and read (for hou can'st read) the lay
> Graved on the stone beneath yon aged thorn."
>
> (Gray T. 1751. "Elegy written in a Country
> Churchyard accessed 17.10.2014)

Such manifestations of grief were, Walter (1999) argues, of help to Puritans in finding an outlet for their grief.:

> " Whereas it is normally argued that romanticism helped foster the death culture of the Victorian era, Draper suggests that romanticism itself drew on the need to speak of mortality and mourning in a culture that eschewed grand requiem masses. In turn, this helped create the Victorian cult of the cemetery."
>
> (Walter 1999:128)

Although bereaved men were permitted, up until the nineteenth century, to cry in public, after that time, due to the influence of French culture, etiquette decreed that men should contain their tears and refrain from crying in public. (Walter 1999:134). This cultural requirement for "a stiff upper lip" was adopted by public schools and was inculcated into generations of "well-educated men". Thus, grief and the outward manifestations of grief, having been vacated by men, became the domain of women. Thus, women limited their social life and appearances in public in order to comfort the bereaved in private. (Walter 1999:134)

By Victorian and Edwardian times, the nursing of the dying fell to women – either relatives, domestic servants or trained nurses They would be expected to be with the dying the whole time. Men, on the other hand, were expected to be in the 'public sphere' (Jalland 1999:98). Once the person had died, then women cared for the dead. They washed and dressed the body ready for others to pay their last respects. (Jalland 1999:212)

In Victorian and Edwardian times, widows would appear to be supported emotionally by female friends and relatives (Jalland 1999, chapter 11). To find oneself a widow, was not only about coping with the death of your husband, but was also a financial loss as well as a status and social loss. Widows whose husbands died penniless were either, in the case of upper or middle-class people, reliant upon any settlement at the time of their marriage or were reliant upon living with a relative. Widowhood was a 'final destiny, an involuntary commitment to a form of social exile' (Jalland 1999:231)

Those widows from working class families found themselves reliant on the Poor Law or charity pay-outs and were totally dependent on their own families. (Jalland 1999:236). What is interesting to note, is that widows rarely remarried compared with widowers. Jalland (1999) also notes the conversations of widows with other women. Most of these were confidences expressed about how they felt being a widow, as for example Lady Wantage in 1905

"One's whole past life seems, as it were, swept away; nothing can mitigate the feeling of solitude and desolation…"

(Jalland 1999:236)

The prospects of remarrying, once the age of 30 had been reached, were few and far between (11.611 out of 1,000), compared with widowers (28.627 out of 1,000) (Jalland 1999:255): the older the widow, the less chance of her remarrying and regaining any sort of social status. Widows were expected to dress in 'full black mourning' (Jalland 1999:300) for two years and in the words of Lou Taylor (Jalland 1999:301):

"the drab, uncomfortable attire symbolised the perception that a wife's identity and sexuality were subsumed in her husband's and died with him' putting her 'beyond the marriage market."

Men's clothes, on the other hand, were much less specific – black mourning cloaks, hat bands, black gloves and cravats were all that were required. (Jalland 1999:301)

It would appear then that the social stigmatisation of becoming a widow far outweighed that of a widower. For the widow, she became reliant on her female friends for both company and solace. The expectation that widows would keep company with their family, women and other widows had one major consequence. We note that both Mrs. Fawcett and Mrs Pankhurst became widows in the nineteenth century and by the end of that century they were in their different ways campaigning vigorously for the emancipation of women and in particular for the franchise for women. (Herstoria 23.06.2012 accessed 26.09.2016). The widower, on the other hand, lost no social status and could, after a period of mourning, resume his normal life. This does not appear to have changed too much today.

All of this seems to be a far cry from 1 Tim 5 (NIV 1984) where the support of widows within the family, or, if the widow has no surviving relatives, the ways in which the church should support them was made explicit. For example, Acts 6:1 (NIV 1984) makes reference to how a food distribution programme for widows was being ignored:

"In those days when the number of disciples was increasing, the Grecian Jews among them complained against the Hebraic Jews because their widows were being overlooked in the daily distribution of food."

This was noted by the disciples and resolved by authorising seven of their number to take responsibility for rectifying this oversight. This resonates with the responsibilities that Jewish children have for grieving parents which were visited in Chapter two.

It is also interesting to note that upper and middle-class women in early and middle Victorian times were not expected to attend funerals (Jalland 1999:221) due to their inability to control their emotions. Novels sometimes enable readers to understand more easily social conventions. In Elizabeth Gaskell's 'Cranford Chronicles' (2007:109), for example, she reports the following:

"The corpse was to be taken from the station to the parish church, there to be interred. Miss Jessie had set her heart on following it to the grave, and no dissuasives could alter her resolve. Her restraint upon herself made her almost obstinate; she resisted all Miss Pole's entreaties, and Miss Jenkyn's advice. At last Miss Jenkyns gave up the point; and after a silence, which I feared portended some deep displeasure against Miss Jessie, Miss Jenkyns said she should accompany the latter to the funeral. 'It is not fit for you to go alone. It would be against both propriety and humanity were I to allow it.'……"

Miss Jenkyns was aware of social conventions, but at the same time felt she had to support Miss Jessie and chose to walk with her, which could have resulted in them both being pariahs within their community. However, rather than allowing Miss Jessie to suffer stigmatisation alone, Miss Jenkyns chose to be with her at her time of need. Again, it is interesting to note the support of one woman for another in the face of adversity.

As we observed earlier, upper and middle-class women were discouraged from attending funerals because of their emotional frailty. However, their male counterparts were allowed to grieve openly but were still expected to control themselves at the funeral and in public; these expectations certainly date back to 1651 when Jeremy Taylor thought that expressing emotion prior to the funeral was acceptable but certainly not during the funeral. (Jalland 1999:221)

In contrast, working class women were allowed to partake in funerals and the subsequent feast (wake) afterwards, and were as a result, supported by their communities; whereas upper and middle-class women were isolated as a result of non-attendance at funerals and the fact that funeral feasts consisted of a little food for those in the immediate family, prior to the reading of the will. Funeral feasts were discouraged in the upper and middle classes (Jalland 1999:223)

Although a public display of grief was frowned upon, it was expected that the bereaved would keep mementos. These varied from photographs, painted pictures to death-masks and keeping a written account of the deceased's life (Jalland 1999:288) More affluent families were able to donate a window in a church as a memorial or purchasing an ornate headstone for the grave (Jalland:291). Prior to 1882 and the second Married Women's Property Act, widows had no independent rights, so often made informal wills bequeathing particular pieces of jewellery or clothes to various people instead. Mourning jewellery became more fashionable with, for example, Mary Ann Rogers leaving 'her granddaughter Annie, aged 9 a brooch containing the hair of her dead baby brother.' (Jalland 1999: 296). Small pieces of furniture or crockery were also often left and passed down from generation to generation in remembrance of the one who had died. Although mourning jewellery has largely gone out of fashion, ordinary pieces of jewellery are, even nowadays, bequeathed to family members. Today family photographs are passed down through the generations and so too, are little personal treasures, such as family china. It is these keepsakes that keep alive our affection and memories of those who have died. On the one hand death becomes a business, but that business sowed ideas that, subsequently, became matters of consensual family grieving. Sometimes the deceased organise the distribution of keepsakes before they die.

Whilst grieving went through a process of marketisation and then remembrances of the deceased became a matter of family negotiation; the body of the deceased became a matter for scientific investigation and then for medical training and finally obsolete so far as the practice of medicine was concerned. Now it seems as if the only value medicine attaches to dead bodies is where consent has been given for the use of body parts to help the living. So, the medical profession stepped forward in caring for the dying while priests were eased into the shadows, leaving little emotional care for either the dying or the bereaved. One response to this emotional tragedy has been the development of hospice care allowing the dying the comfort of their home and families. Hospice carers became the new workers for death caring for both the dying and the bereaved, often sustaining contact for some period after the funeral. New developments in medical science mean that doctors concentrate more on the symptoms of the patient, than the patient as a whole with the result that the doctors are becoming less foregrounded. Compassionate care is increasingly becoming available through the hospice movement who are sensitive to the spiritual needs of both the dying and the bereaved. We can see that the wheel is turning again and the human aspects of death are once more moving to the foreground.

Returning to the late nineteenth and early twentieth century, those in more affluent families would expect nurses or servants or both to lay out the body. Instructions for the laying out fell mainly to women (Jalland 212) and predominantly to the nurses who were expected to guide the other members of the household. An instructions pamphlet (1910) was written by two

Queen's nurses, to guide other women on the laying out the dead. Even today, there are instructions on what to do with those who have died in hospital. However, today's instructions do not include saying a Christian prayer in view of the fact that Britain is recognisably more culturally diverse than in late Edwardian times. (Jalland 212)

Since the times of Miss Jessie and Miss Jenkyns, the engagement of the English public with the Anglican church has steadily declined. Without wishing to comment on well-aired theories of secularisation we want to note that in 1851 40% of the population attended a Sunday service at an Anglican church. By 2000, this had diminished to below 7.5%. Anglican baptisms in 1900 dropped from about 65% to just above 27% in 1993. (Coffey J. Secularisation: is it inevitable? Accessed 24.10.2014)

There were changes in the formal rites associated with death and concomitant grief but we know little if anything of the impact these changes had on the bereaved. From the mid-1870's there was recognisable pressure to reform mourning rituals emanating from the National Funeral and Mourning Reform Association (Jalland 1999: 371) which advocated simpler mourning attire and a reduced length of mourning time. Arnold Bennett in his book "The Old Wives' Tale" (1908) talks about Constance's experiences of bereavement. Her husband's funeral was 'simple' and 'private' according to his wishes. Bennett places the simplicity of the funeral as mirrored in Constance's simple and abbreviated mourning. Although Constance acknowledges that the death of her husband is an 'amputation', she reasons with herself that marriage always ends with the death of one or the other partner and that this is a fact of life. She regards herself as being very fortunate in having been married for twenty-one years to a caring and decent man.

As well as mourning ritual changes, there were changes in the practical arrangements. Crematoria were established as being legal in 1885, although cremations, never illegal, were formally recognised as being legal in 1902. (Jalland 1999:205) This Act reflected the gradual rise in acceptability, with

1,000 cremations being carried out by 1911. However, it has to be noted that it was not until the 1960's that cremations became more typical with half of those dying being cremated (Jalland 1999:205.) The rise in acceptability of cremations must be acknowledged as a European phenomenon with only 8% of funerals being linked with cremation in the United States (Shillace 2015:199).

These changes in custom and ritual were accentuated by the Great War. As a result of one in eight men being killed and one in four being wounded (Jalland: 1999:372) 'it was argued that national morale and patriotism would suffer if thousands of widows all wore full mourning dress, especially after the mass deaths from 1916. Because of the huge death toll of the Great War, obviously every family would have been dressed in black (Jalland 1999:372) However, D.C. Coleman (cited Jalland, 1999:371) noted that there was a move away from wearing black crepe for mourning from the 1880's onwards which was accelerated after Queen Victoria's death in 1901.

The Great War's impact on the nation was so intense that in 1920 a move was made by Revd David Railton to repatriate an unknown soldier's remains back to England. The Unknown Soldier was entombed in Westminster Abbey on 11th November 1920. An ecumenical Christian service was held before the body left France. However, the body of the unknown soldier could be from any of the Armed Forces and indeed from any part of the United Kingdom, the Dominions or Colonies (Unknown Warrior – Westminster Abbey accessed 24.10.2014) so there is a possibility that the Christian service could have been for a soldier of another faith. What is apparent is the need for a place for people to visit whose menfolk were never repatriated, and in creating the Tomb of the Unknown Solider, this need was fulfilled. Perhaps an unintended consequence of this process was that the Anglican church and British Establishment had bestowed the utmost dignity and respect on a soldier who could have been of any denomination or faith.

The Cenotaph together with the battlefield graves, the Thiepval Memorial to the missing of the Somme battlefields and the Menin Gate may well have provided greater comfort to the bereaved than the letters of condolence which they received. Such letters with their rhetoric of patriotism and glory in which most people had lost faith, simply seemed to underline, as Jalland (1999:372) says:

"the hopelessness of the bereaved and the declining stocks of sympathy and energy among overworked family and community"

The First World War meant that families and friends were compelled to come to terms with the huge numbers of 'violent and unnatural deaths' (Jalland 1999:372). As a result, Christian rituals of mourning were found to be less supportive than in Victorian times. Men were killed and left dead in the mud of French and Belgian battlefields. The bodies of the alleged enemies, their officers and their common-foot soldiers were indistinguishable from each other. Those bodies that were found were buried in graves with the epitaph "A Soldier of the Great War". This war democratised death by robbing the bereaved of any certainty about the cause of death and the location of the bodies of their loved ones. It also made it impossible to distinguish between officers and men in the treatment of those bodies that were repatriated. As Jalland observes (1999:373) "Christian parents found great difficulty in reconciling their faith with the premature loss of their children (and husbands) "

In 1918, the Spanish 'flu pandemic added to the pressures on families and communities. 228,000 died in Britain alone and overall, in the world, it killed three times the number killed in the First World War (The Spanish flu pandemic of 1918 accessed 24.10.2014) It disproportionately killed more twenty to thirty-year old people than those who were older, frailer or unhealthy. Although the 'flu was brought back from the trenches it now affected both women and men, further adding to national grief. It is difficult to gauge the impact of this pandemic on the work of the church in relation to grief since we have found records to be extremely slim. As Paul comments (2015:218) the idealised Victorian family death "was shattered when confronted with the epic slaughter of the battlefield and the wards of the dying. This left an indelible scar on the conscience of an entire generation."

Similar horrors were revisited twenty-five years later in the Second World War where not only were the armed forces, but also civilians targeted, particularly those in the industrial heartlands and transport hubs. During the Blitz in the U.K. alone, 32,000 civilians were killed in Britain, with 87,000 being seriously injured. Over a thousand Anglican churches were destroyed in the Second World War. Men left for the front; women for agriculture and industry, hence many a cleric lost both his church and his congregation. (Spinks cited in Prochaska F. The Church of England the Collapse of Christian Charity accessed 24.10.2014)

Consequently, in the late 1940's there was one priest for 5,000 people in London, Liverpool and Manchester (Garbett cited in Prochaska accessed 24.10.2014) With so many people in his parish it became extremely difficult and often impossible to exercise Christian charity leading to a reassessment of church policy. As Paul (2015:218) observes:

"Following the developments of effective treatments, dying switched to being a secular event controlled by doctors, and the Church duly surrendered its leading role."

Garbett (cited in Prochaska accessed 24.10.2014) declared the welfare state embodied "the Law of Christ". The Anglican hierarchy had turned Jesus into a Socialist. The introduction of the welfare state with medical care available to all by need rather than by wealth, meant that opportunities for the preservation of life were now available to everyone.

As it becomes increasingly medical teams rather than clerics, who are present at the moment of death, and as guidance to nurses illustrates, the washing and laying out of the dead becomes the domain of the hospital rather than the family. Although institutionalised by the medical profession, we suggest that, with few exceptions, caring for the body of the deceased and first contact with the bereaved, confirming the sorrow of a loved one's death, remains steadfastly (nurses) women's work.

It would seem that parish priests leave the work of visiting the sick to hospital chaplains and parishioners visiting their friends and acquaintances in hospital. The hospice movement, however, offers a homelier, less medicalised environment for the dying and their families, as has been discussed earlier. An Anglican priest might well find her/himself comforting distressed relatives over the outcome of an illness they had not witnessed. For the bereaved and the priest, therefore, there is a void. This hole in a Christian vision of dying was as Paul (2015:219) says, filled "by the medical model......notably the ubiquitous work of Elizabeth Kubler-Ross."

Kramarae (2000:300) reminds us that, even today, looking after elderly, ill or dying relatives has 'fallen into the hands of single women who were thought to have more time for it'; even though they may have a full-time job and other commitments. No mention is made of the time single men may have for caring. This may be because any outside work done by women is not deemed to be as important as a man's (or perhaps as well paid); it may be because in general women are more compassionate; or it may be because there is still this remaining vestige where women are 'expected' to be the person running the home and so capable of caring for the infirm or terminally ill.

In 2005 the Archbishops Council in its review of the legislation for parochial fees reported that Anglican ministers conducted 207,200 funerals compared with officiating at 57,200 weddings, which is approximately four funerals to every one marriage. (Archbishops' Council: Four funerals and a wedding accessed 24.10.2014)

In 2013 the Church of England statistics estimated that 33% (160,000 annually) of funerals were undertaken by an ordained minister of the

Anglican church. (Statistics for Mission 2013 accessed 24.10.2014) We suspect that, for many people, experiencing the shock of bereavement, they know of no other place to turn. Funeral directors also have a list of people they can turn to if the bereaved are unsure. This list primarily consists of ordained and lay ministers. We also recognise that local churches frequently cherish the oldest members of their congregations as part of their church family. In such circumstances, it is very natural for the minister to conduct the funeral service.

These statistics show that the taking of funerals predominates over baptisms and marriages, with the Church of England offering funerals as a pastoral service. However, there is a question over the capacity of the church to offer the bereaved sustained pastoral support. By capacity we mean the willingness, the competence, the kindness and the compassion to empathise with the bereaved.

This definition of capacity leads us to enquire and reflect on the experience of both ministers in their training and the bereaved in their loss.

Indeed, the experience of both the parishioners and their clergy may have led to keeping grief at a 'safe distance'. For the ordinary members of a congregation, it may be as Paul (2015:211) suggests that whilst local churches may offer guidance "on the theological issues surrounding our mortality and after life….. enquiries concerning the support of the dying are frequently outsourced to hospital or hospice chaplains as if ministers prefer to focus on family or social projects, treating 'dying' itself as an exotic event."

Paul (2015) goes on to intimate that admission to hospices is itself based on medical rather than spiritual recommendations. In some senses then, dying has been outsourced from the parish clergy and medicalised beyond their reach. None the less contemporary theologians e.g. Fiddes (2015:235) points us towards a theology of grief:

"There can be no standard formula to meet the diversity of circumstances and human needs, but we can cultivate an increasing harmony with the rhythms of love in the triune God that re-shape death into a servant."

Part of the medicalisation of life is the medicalisation of death and hence organisations who care for those who are dying may offer guidance on grieving for those left behind. There is a recognition in the literature given to the bereaved that the end of an individual's life is a unique event and thus their response will also be unique. Many end of life organisations offer guidance to those who are grieving that suggests they may feel numbness, denial, anger, depression and finally acceptance. (for example, Macmillan, accessed 01.11.2014, Marie Curie, accessed 01.11.2014 and Cruse accessed 01.11.2014). Readers will recognise this as the Kubler-Ross account and some sources go further than offering this account and suggest that we may also grieve for the loss of caring for a loved one, which may leave a huge void in the bereaved person's life. Most agencies offer support services for the bereaved and some suggest a possible contact with a spiritual or faith leader. Compassion, as a result, appears to have become 'specialised' and the 'specialism' does not necessarily include Anglican clergy. It seems to separate grief into an industry such as the business of funerals and the cost of an undertaker, as well as the cost of using a minister or other leader to take the service.

The public moments of grief are cared for by the clergy (often Anglican) and the private moments of grief are outsourced to specialist agencies. Surely these phenomena were unintended. So, too, might be the traces of a life well lived that can be found on the internet. We are still "linked in" to friends who have died, their Facebook pages still exist and are sometimes used as a site where others may record their grief. Sometimes the grief is for a friend or relative and at other times it is part of a public sharing of grief, for example the thousands of young people who tweeted their grief after the Columbine massacres. Contemporary communications media can turn private grief into public grief. In the United Kingdom, this was clearly visible at the death of

Princess Diana as well as in the London bombings of 2005 and the Twin Towers collapse in New York in 2009. Messages and flowers are sometimes left at what become public sites of grief by friends and strangers alike. These things say something about our readiness to participate in the grief of others and to express our grief at the personal losses of others. There is evidence here of a willingness to accommodate grief and sharing personal feelings with unknown others.

In this chapter, we began with some reflection on relationships between wealth and the length of life in England. For many, poverty continued to rob them of any hope of longevity. For the wealthy, and indeed for the poor, particular risks of mortality, for men, were warfare, and for women, were childbirth. Women continued to prepare the dead for burial although by the end of the Tudor era, coffin makers were employed by the wealthier people who would in turn bring in local women to prepare the body for burial. Other than this, we saw no marked changes in the role of women in burials and mourning between 1509 and 1688. If anything, there was a continuing trend for distinctions in life to be carried into distinctions in death. Legislation was introduced for the care of the poor, who would have necessarily included the widows from lower middle and working-class families. The Poor Relief (The 1662 Poor Relief Act accessed 01.11.2014) was gathered and distributed by parish, reinforcing clear distinctions between the 'haves' and the 'have nots'. On death, those on 'the parish' were afforded a pauper's funeral. So, while friends may have provided a wake which working class women would attend, the burial was a simple affair in an unmarked grave.

Changes in legislation permitted the practice of other Protestant faith traditions (1689) and of the Roman Catholic faith (1829) (Living Heritage: key dates 1689 to 1829 accessed01.11.2014) There appears to be an interplay between wealth, power and faith that was implicated in burial and grief. The fashion for wooden coffins and deeper graves in the eighteenth century meant that monuments and memorials became more popular. Social distinctions remained with the public display of sympathy by the middle classes being endorsed by the 1760's. By the 1800's, death, as we have seen, was increasingly medicalised with a focus on prolonging life rather than the care of the soul. We noted that the expectations of middle and upper-class grief in the Victorian era, were particularly onerous for women. They were expected to observe formal mourning for two years and unless they were under thirty were unlikely to marry again. They became dependent on their families and grief gave way to social stigma. Working and lower middle-class widows were subject to the horrific changes in Poor Relief of 1834 (Higginbotham P. accessed 12.01.2015) that saw the establishment of the Workhouse. Widows were separated from their sons and along with their daughters undertook tasks suited to the labouring poor.

Towards the end of the Victorian era, all women went to funerals which was a change for middle and upper-class women. By 1900, women were increasingly involved in the laying out of the dead. The massive increase in male deaths with the onset of the First World War, saw a simplification of the use of mourning clothes. This simplification prevailed throughout the First World War and continued so that by the end of the Spanish flu epidemic it became the custom. Most widows would have adopted dark clothing, certainly in the period immediately following the death of a loved one. For men, a black armband and a black tie were deemed appropriate. This period was marked by a continuing transition of care of the dying and thus of the bereaved from the ecclesiastical to the medical. The introduction of the National Health Service in 1948 saw the democratisation of health care and the end of the workhouse.

5

GATHERING DATA; INTERVIEWS AND REFLECTING ON INTERVIEWS. ANALYSING TEXTS THAT DESCRIBE VOCATIONAL TRAINING AND EDUCATION

METHODOLOGICAL, PRACTICAL THEOLOGY AND QUALITATIVE RESEARCH.

JUST AS WE have acknowledged that every death is a unique experience for the deceased's family, so too, we want to suggest that for each family member grief will be a unique experience. Consider, for example, the anomaly of an individual who, although, grieving deeply, seems unable to embrace the grief of other members of the family. This kind of self-focussed grief might be thought of as unusual and perhaps it is, but what it certainly does is demand that we return to and reflect on the Kubler-Ross formula and consider its generalisability. For the sympathetic priest, it poses a particular conundrum of how to include those whose exclusion might produce a more compassionate farewell to the deceased.

Consider, too, the surviving spouse who is afflicted with Alzheimer's disease. One day the bereaved may be overwhelmed with a sense of loss and able to do little other than weep for twenty-four hours or more. Following this intense, but brief period of grieving, a bereaved spouse with Alzheimer's disease may then confuse the death of their most cherished loved one with other deaths in their past. Hence they pass almost seamlessly from Kubler-Ross' stage of numbness (and denial) to acceptance without traversing any of the intermediate stages.

Here we have provided a couple of illustrations which resist the group classification of bereavement behaviours. In our analysis, we will attempt to treat respectfully, each shared narrative as a deeply personal and unique account of the compassion of others as it articulates with a bereavement. We are acknowledging the uniqueness of each individual's experience of grief and of grief within a family and community. This acknowledgement might well also include the uniqueness of the experience for the minister serving the family. Nonetheless, Anglican ministers undertake their duties with a sense of certainty in the Triune God and the Resurrection. We shall return to this certainty later in this chapter.

When we speak of each shared narrative, we mean the accounts that we have elicited from bereaved spouses who, to a greater or lesser degree, may have had some association with the Anglican church. As will become apparent, sometimes this connection was, in the first instance, simply for help with funeral arrangements.

We are concerned with a two-fold exploration of narratives about the death of a loved spouse that can be associated with the work of the Anglican ministry. First, we are interested in the narratives of those who have lost a loved spouse and received some form of support from the Anglican church. Secondly, we want to understand how ministers are prepared for their responsibilities towards the bereaved in their parish. To explore this, we shall undertake a textual analysis of materials describing the preparation for ministry offered by training colleges in England.

To analyse the former, we shall reflect on the narratives that have been garnered from our sample. These narratives have been gathered using a semi-structured dialogic interview. This approach is usually described as a qualitative method. We aimed to understand the reasons why bereaved spouses find certain people's help beneficial, thereby answering the "why?" and "how?" questions. We acknowledge that this method has required us to confine our research to far fewer people (a limited group of bereaved spouses) than survey methods would allow. We recognise that our approach has been time-consuming since both respectful interview and respectful analysis has taken considerable time. Although time-consuming and employing a small opportunity sample, it will take us some way towards answering the question "Is Grief a Women's Room?" Certainly, as Schillace (2015:12) proposes "sharing our stories provides hope and community, so that none of us needs face death alone and in the silent dark". Thus, the solace and integrity offered by a "women's room" might similarly be offered by the comfort of narratives of loss and support, such as those here provided. The research approach adopted is ethically, ontologically and epistemologically aligned with the principal foci of our enquiries. Earlier in this chapter, we spoke of the certainty that Anglican ministers have. In addition, to this certainty, we carry a sense of Anglican compassion. When we are prioritising our ethical stance, and understanding what it is to minister to the grieving, then ontologically (following Nodding 1984) we are concerned with 'one cared for and one caring', hence epistemologically we are committed to a caring investigation of compassion. Hence our approach to semi-structured interviewing in relation to death and grieving is informed by both a rational commitment to compassion and the Anglican certainties of a Triune God and of the Resurrection.

A question for practical feminist theology concerns carrying these certainties into a world of uncertainty and a rejection of grand narratives. Graham, in 1996, cited in Osmer (2008:157), offers a response to this question when she asserts "all values, sources and norms are understood as validated and generated in purposeful action (praxis) toward liberation". The second challenge to data arising from dialogic interviewing, as it articulates with practical theology concerns the uncertainties of data in contrast with the certainties of faith. Pattison (Swinton and Mowat

2006:80ff) suggests a spirit of open dialogue which genuinely seeks after truth and respects the perspectives offered by other disciplines. His model of theological reflection as a mutual critical conversation involves a dynamic relationship between each of the following pairs: 'experience' with 'situational exploration', 'situational exploration' with theological exploration/reflection'; theological exploration/reflection' with 'revised practice' and 'revised practice with experience'.

In our work, experience is represented through dialogical interviews with bereaved spouses, situational exploration is represented in our commentaries on these. Our theological exploration and reflection can be found in Chapters 3, 13 and 14. It is in these latter chapters that our suggestions for revised practice can be found.

At this point it is appropriate to shed a little light on what we are referring to when we speak of understanding grief and the status of death and subsequent care within the Anglican church. We shall be sharing two kinds of data: the first of these will come from our interviews with informants whose life partner has died and who are prepared to talk about that experience with us. We are indebted to them for their courage and candour. This then places responsibilities on researchers to respect their stories.

Secondly, we will conduct a brief analysis of the textual accounts of the training of ordinands. We shall be looking to see how far this training enables ordinands to guide and sustain bereaved people in their parish. On the basis of these two analyses, we shall be making some suggestions about understandings of grief and grieving and of the potential of academic and personal enrichment of the training of ordinands.

WHY INTERVIEWS?

We have selected interviews as our method, because we believe they will help us to acknowledge the differences between informants and the distinctiveness of their responses. Wengraf (2001:1) reminds us that interviews are a particular kind of research conversation. Kvale and Brinkmann (2009:1) clarify that such conversations "attempt to understand the world from the subject's point of view, to unfold the meaning of their experiences, to uncover their lived world prior to scientific explanations." As well as the cultivation of conversational skills, both texts raise the question of scientific interpretation. We are not especially interested in objectifying the voices of our informants; rather we want to recognise the nuances and distinctiveness of their responses. Having said this, we also believe that it would be irresponsible to ignore commonalities where they occur.

HOW TO INTERVIEW?

Just as we have argued, there can be no entirely normal death and hence no entirely normal grief, we do not believe there can be a normal process for interviewing. We entered each interview with a set of semi-structured, fluid, open-ended questions. By semi-structured, we mean that we had identified a probable set of questions and sequenced them, but that these questions and this sequence were adapted by us in the light of our informants' responses. By open-ended, we mean we asked what our informants thought or felt about their experiences. We could not possibly know the answers to such questions before our interview conversation. By fluid, we mean that the sequence and specifics of our questions were not always identical or necessarily especially similar. The sequence and content of questions was adapted.

During each interview conversation then, we adapted our open-ended questions and the way we asked them in response to our informants' answers. This process allowed our informants to change the direction of the interview asking formal or supplementary questions and close the interview as and when they felt appropriate. Our interviews were always close to conversation and never interrogational. We therefore opted for open-ended, semi-structured, dialogic interviews. In many respects, this appears to be directly comparable with the field work component of the research undertaken by the Stroebes (personal communication 17.05.2015). In keeping with our theorised position, we worked hard to ensure that the questions we asked and the interjections we used were what we would describe as gently dialogic rather than robustly challenging. For example, "Did Janet organise the flowers?"; It's the little things.."; "Safeguarding yourself?"; "Bit like Jack Spratt…" ; "A symbol of eternal love.." Each of these is an example of interviewer responses that elicited further detail from an informant. They are each part of the dialogue developed in specific interviews.

In our experience interviews that focus on bereavement and grieving take the interviewee to a very emotional and often distressing place. This places the interviewee in an undeniably stressful conversation and simultaneously takes the interviewer back to their own experiences. So the work of interviewing is emotionally demanding for both participants and, if power lies with the interviewer, requires a deeply and unavoidably empathetic approach to the interviews. Our ownership of the emotional territory we were visiting demanded, in our opinion, that we adopt an open, malleable approach to our interviews. We began with the kind of open-ended interview discussed by Kvale and Brinkmann (2009:130). There was indeed a "guide that included an outline of topics to be covered with suggested questions". As they go on to explain it is possible that it is "the interviewer's judgement and tact decides how closely to stick to the guide and how much to follow up the interviewees answers and the new directions they may open up." This approach to interviewing is usually described as semi-structured.

We hope that it is transparent that we are engaged in "empathetic interviewing" Kvale and Brinkmann (2009:148) which implies "taking a stance in favour of those studied". We contend that alongside being empathetic our interviews are also discursive in that we are comfortable with the interviewee defining the discourse; although in some ways we were also concerned to seek out where the power to sustain was embedded within our informants' discourses. This approach with its variation in questions and the way they are posed in response to the interviewee's responses is usually described as discursive or dialogic interviewing.

For a full version of our initial attempt at a guide for interviewing, based on reading and conversations with colleagues see appendix A. The flexibility with which we treated this guide should be apparent from the interviews which we present in full in subsequent chapters of this book.

We informally canvassed potential informants and having established their initial willingness to help us with our enquiry we went on to explain that they would decide the time and place of interview. They would also have control over the final anonymised transcript that emerged from our dialogue and were directed towards a trained counsellor should their distress call for one. The physical arrangements and the undertakings we provided about control of the data, control over physical interview arrangements and our respect for the interviewed all recognised and valued the interviewed persons' contribution and control over their data. As can be seen from our guide, interviewees were assured that although the interviews would be recorded, their anonymity would be retained and the transcripts kept on a password protected computer, with the audio recordings being deleted.

We were not going to deliberately enquire into the ways in which their immediate families supported or helped, but rather we wanted to learn more about the ways in which those outside the immediate family helped or supported the bereaved. We were not using focus groups because we wanted to learn about each individual's experience of support and help and were aware that focus groups can sometimes shift personal thinking. We interviewed people using our guide of open-ended questions and voice recorded them, with their consent, noting down any extra gestures/non-verbal communications. We added these back into our transcripts after they had been produced for us and checked by us. We left open the opportunity to return to our informants in order to clarify issues they may have raised.

WHO TO INTERVIEW?

We have already identified some exclusions from our sample, these being those who seem to be unable to comprehend their loss for medical reasons and those who seem to be unable to comprehend the scale of another's loss for personal reasons. We are also deliberately excluding those who are not formally married and without a legal attachment. In an age which seems to treat death as an exotic event it may seem strange or ironic, but we are seeking to interview those who came to grieve through a "medically normal" experience of death and who used the services of the Anglican church. They were all bereaved more than two years ago. Giving the bereaved 'space' means important anniversaries have been experienced, and although probably still grieving, we feel that this space will make it just a little bit easier for them to discuss their experiences. The space offered by the passing of time may also make it easier for them to give us a bigger, personal picture. Here we are excluding spouses of those who have died in battle or have committed suicide. Neither, at this stage, will we be seeking interviews from those who have participated in assisted dying.

From this small personal sample, we will be able to identify a group of people who supported those who were bereaved. In terms of our ontology – some of the 'ones caring'.

HOW MANY TO INTERVIEW?

While it can be argued (Baker & Edwards 2012) that the number of interviews necessary for any project will vary with the nature and scope of the project itself we are following the position adopted by Guest et al (2006) that saturation (no new material arises) occurs within the first twelve interviews. Guest et al also note that no new underpinning themes reflecting taken for granted social underpinnings (metathemes) arise after six interviews. Since it is our intention to explore the limits of existing constructions of bereavement and grief and point towards new ways of conceptualising the way assistance might be proffered by Anglican ministers, we consider seven interviews reflects the scale of our exploration.

REFLECTING ON INTERVIEWS

We have aspired to bring a refreshing outlook towards our interviews. We have both reflected on power and purpose in educational discourses and we have adopted different approaches in this work. One of us looked at "Supporting children with additional needs" (Lee in Davies J.D. et al 1998); and "Stories Children Tell" Lee et al in Pollard A. ed.1987) and the other has looked at discourse analysis and specialised in the analysis of classroom utterances (Eke et al 2005) and more recently in work adjacent to this looked at "Kindness in early childhood" (Butcher & Eke 2013).

In this book, we have reflected on the often moving accounts of bereavement and associated personal grief that we have collected. We are reluctant to try and push this reflection into pre-existing patterns so whilst mindful of Kubler-Ross, the Stroebes and critiques of their works, for example, Schillace (2015), we will not be claiming any special "scientific" insight.

We have not sought to use seven interviews to provide a grand meta-narrative of bereavement and grieving within the sphere of the Anglican church in the U.K. This means that we have treated each interview transcription as an entity in its own right. Where there are links between our interpretations of individual transcripts, we recognise that these are products of our own reflection rather than substantial pre-existing matters of fact.

The interviews are a matter of co-construction between interviewers and interviewed. This is reflected in the way we have presented our interview data in the form of a script with very occasional "stage directions". All of the utterances were comprehendable and there were no ambiguities in the representation of the spoken word. A professional transcriber was employed and we checked the printed record alongside the spoken record before sending it in an anonymised form to the interviewee for ratification. Each script has been presented as a separate chapter. We will comment on the script, drawing on our individual experiences of our reflecting on language. In so doing, we have aimed to enrich the meanings our informants have given us. We have made this process transparent by providing the full text of each interview in italic script and our comments are inserted in standard form. Since we have intended to let the scripts speak for themselves, we have not juggled the order in which they were collected.

COURSE OUTLINES:

We collected the on-line information published by colleges training Anglican priests. We sought to use only information that was in the public domain. We analysed this information by searching it for a range of terms that we thought significant. Thus, we searched for bereavement, grieving, compassion for the bereaved and funerals. We are comfortable using this kind of textual analysis because it will not be used on its own and the outcomes will be woven in to our perceptions of productive ways to support those seeking ordination particularly in Anglican or Episcopalian churches. (see Fairclough 2003)

6

AMY'S STORY

INTRODUCTION:

WE ARE COMMITTED to valuing the voices of our informants and hence we have presented as faithfully as we can (within the limits of protecting anonymity) the accounts given to us by those informants who were both generous and courageous enough to relive with us some of the most distressing times of their lives. We recognise that being interviewed and asked to summon back moments when their loved ones died was emotionally draining for our informants. Whilst we ought to have been able to anticipate that interviewing our informants would be emotionally demanding for us, we also have to acknowledge that reflecting on the transcripts of those interviews was emotionally taxing.

Readers will find the fullest version we are able to offer of our informants' accounts. We have chosen to offer a commentary within those accounts so that the origins of our claims in the voices of informants are transparent.

At the end of each informant's narrative we attempt to draw together strands that we found in each interview.

INTERVIEW WITH AMY WITH EMBEDDED COMMENTARY:

INTRODUCTION:

This interview was the first we conducted and gave us the opportunity to reflect on both the outcomes of the interview and the process itself.

> *Int: What happened after James died? Which people outside your family helped you most during those difficult days?*

These two questions are coupled together. They imply that death and outside assistance are coupled together. They also acknowledge, or perhaps, pre-define, the immediate difficulties individuals face following the death of a loved one

> *Amy: There were instances which remain very clear in my mind about what happened after James died. The consultants had us in to talk about James – and to say that they would give him blood for the next hour (he was haemorrhaging and they couldn't stop it) but that it would be difficult after that. I can remember turning to one of the consultants – she was nearly in tears, and I held her arm and said, "You're doing this really well – have you been on a Bereavement course?" How daft was that?*

This tells us that our informant was familiar with hospital settings and official roles within them. It also tells us that our informant was familiar with the impact that death has on the staff in hospitals and knew of the relevant courses available to help staff to cope in these situations. It is important to note that it was a woman consultant that our informant especially remembered. It also shows that with the benefit of hindsight she is able to reflect on her own response to the shock of bereavement (How daft was that?)

> *Amy: But I also asked if I could wash him, which was an unusual request apparently but for me normalised the situation. If James had been at home, I'd have washed him. I can remember talking to him throughout*

and it just seemed natural to talk to him, in much the same way I always talk to anyone who has died.

Again, the informant tells us that she is familiar with bereavement and how she has responded in the past to others in a similar situation.

Amy: For me it cut out the medicalisation of the situation – it made it more natural I suppose, and certainly more compassionate. Just because someone is dying or has died doesn't mean they aren't a person anymore. The affection for them doesn't die with them.

Here the interviewee has linked knowledge of the manner in which death arrives in modern society and also demonstrates a very personal response to such treatment. It ties this analysis to a very human personal and affectionate response to the death of a loved one.

Amy: The nurse who turned the television screens on to Privacy and Dignity is also a particularly poignant memory I have…..I knew what she was doing and what was happening. The time she said we (my daughters and I) might want to hold his hand…..and I knew what she was saying. Then those final words "He's passed on." I wanted to ask, "Where to?" or to say "Don't be daft – just be honest. Say he's died, that's being honest."

Again, the interviewee tells that she is familiar with hospital procedure at the point of death. Again, she links a very personal moment with a robust critique of practice. Clearly there is something about the phrase "passed on" that carries too much weight for our informant. Perhaps she acknowledges a diversity of belief that goes beyond ideas of "passing on". Describing this behaviour as "daft" seems to acknowledge that the use of the phrase "passed on" is a coping strategy for those dealing with medicalised end of life care.

Amy: And then the ward clerk who just looked at me with such sympathy, saying "It's always worse when it happens to one of us"

This is a personal statement from a member of staff who was present in a formal role acknowledging the 'inclusive family' that the staff of a hospital make. For our respondent, this hospital death was a death shared with a community of care.

> *Amy: We left shortly afterwards and went home. I think I sat at the kitchen table trying to eat something but finding it impossible. Charles came round; sat me down and just let me talk. I kept saying it was so sad – but he persuaded me to say, "I am just so sad". But, I didn't think it was strictly correct – the whole situation was so sad. It was sad for everyone. It was sad that such an academic, thinking outside the box sort of person, should have died. It was sad our daughters' children would never know their grandpa. That was all sad.*

This informant is prioritising the consequences for her extended family over immediate personal consequences and the respondent seems to feel that Charles is trying to impose a preferred reading on Amy's response and that has been corrected. Amy speaks of 'our daughters' when speaking of shared loss.

> *Amy: I remember my head and mouth aching from crying so much. Our daughters were all with me as well as Tom and Nancy, some close friends. They left the following day and then I had to think carefully. We were due to have visitors from the Caribbean staying with us, so my first priority was to e-mail them to tell them what had happened and to ensure arrangements had been made for them to stay elsewhere.*

The physical consequences of grief have stayed with this informant as well as the need to deal with everyday matters. In shared grief Amy speaks of 'our daughters' which is as if James is still part of the unfolding event.

> *Amy: The transplant team rang the next day and were so kind – James was on the donor list, so that was all sorted out.*

Here we have a recollection of a significant practical arrangement which met the wishes of James.

> *Amy: I think people rang, but Jo put them off from coming round. The Wednesday was all a blur. Caroline (a minister) came round in the afternoon – with two carrier bags full of cakes. "You'll need those, Amy, trust me you really will." She stayed for about half an hour ….and she was right, we did need those cakes! Diana also called round – from college days – she stayed for about twenty minutes which was just right.*

The respondent is acknowledging that she was in receipt of appropriate and sensitive care from female clergy and from a former College friend. Timing would also appear to be an important factor for Amy as she makes special mention of 'twenty minutes being just right'. Amy also acknowledges how appropriate Caroline's gift of cakes was.

> *Amy: On the Thursday I went with the girls to Patient Affairs to collect the medical certificate and the people in there were kind…as was the Registrar…but they have experience of dealing with bereaved people.*

Amy comments on the reactions of the hospital staff both to her and to her daughters emphasising how kind they all were.

> *Amy: The funeral directors were very kind too. We saw Bob, so I said I wanted him buried in the memorial gardens and that I wanted them to sort it all out. That was when Bob said, "No pressure there then Amy!" The Friday we went to the memorial gardens and chose a place for him to be buried under an apple tree. The sun was shining right on the spot and all three of us chose it …it just seemed so fitting. I think it was Jo who said, "It'll be like being in bunk beds, mum…only you'll have the top bunk"!….it is a double grave.*

Amy remembers particularly the kindness of the funeral director who knew her and was comfortable enough with her to share a joke. Again, the informant speaks of the involvement of her daughters in the practicalities of the funeral and they, too, were able to make a small joke.

Amy: Then we hit the weekend....and visitors started to come round.

*The next week was a total blur...the Monday was the day Lionel from the Caribbean was being given his honorary Masters' degree....Norman came and picked me up; Josie met me at the Cathedral and whisked me away for a gown; then I seemed to be surrounded by Norman, Josie, Jake, Jack and June...it was almost like being protected which I really appreciated. I stayed long enough to clap Lionel when he came out of the Cathedral and say a few words to him before leaving with Josie. We went to the local hotel for afternoon tea. I couldn't have managed any more at the Cathedral – that **was** sad. James would have been so jubilant at Lionel getting a degree – I stood up and clapped him as I knew James would have done that.*

Firstly, Amy speaks of social interaction as a blur, then as protective care and again, she reflects on respecting James' wishes.

Amy: That evening I went out with Linda for dinner with Lionel, Chloe and Reg and Joanne, Jack, Jake, Rex and Elizabeth and Anne. It was small enough to be manageable but not so intimate that you felt obliged to say anything. That was probably the hardest day.

Amy reflects on her first personal engagement at which James would have been present. She appreciated that she was not expected to contribute very much to any conversation, but we also note that it was the 'hardest day' so far.

Amy: The following week was filled with visitors. Gillian from work came round which was just lovely – it was she who had done a blessing on James and Jo and I both anointed him. Jill also came round with Daniel; Vera visited; Julia and Dan came; Emmeline popped by; Leanne visited; Joshua from church visited…he said "I've not done many of these visits before.." so I went and made him a cup of tea and landed up talking about him and his dad.

Amy mentions by name the people who came to visit her which would appear to be very significant for her. It is interesting to note that twice as many named visitors were women. We can note here that extended comments are provided for Gillian and for Joshua. We note that Joshua confessed to a lack of experience and allowed Amy to make tea for him and for her to listen to his personal concerns.

Amy: Mike and Jacob called round with cakes. Jacob had made them… which was really sweet. Susan came round a lot. It seemed as if the house was constantly full and predominantly of women.

Here two men offer cakes, again – gifts to share. There is a special recollection for a woman friend here.

Amy: At the weekend Karen flew in from America and Ella, Cora, Dave and Margaret all came. It was especially lovely having Karen there….we go back a long way and as her husband said "You're soul sisters" which we are,

Amy obviously has a very close relationship with Karen and savoured her husband's comment. We also see another group of named visitors arriving.

Int: Can you remember what those people who supported you most said or did that made that special difference? Are you still being supported by those people?

Amy: It wasn't so much sympathy that was given out so much as empathy and practical support. Support from Linda in sorting out somewhere for Lionel and Chloe to say…they visited as well and met Adam, the grandson that James met and I've got a picture of him holding him….which was wonderful. The endless supply of cakes was essential – and there were flowers too…. flowers from Leanne; flowers from the hospital….as well as others. And yes, I am still being supported by those people. Susan has been invaluable…I can just go round there and stand on her doorstep and she knows when a cup of tea is needed, a talk, a cry and a hug….and similarly I do the same for her.

Practical support was an important feature for Amy, but at the same time the kindnesses and compassion were really valued. It is interesting to note that Amy comments on the reciprocal arrangement that she and Susan have in managing grief.

Amy: Ayleen rang every week just to check I was O.K. after he died. The house was just full of visitors….mostly women…and I can remember going back to work saying the house was like a women's room..

Again, Amy comments on the number of visitors who came who were women and names one female person in particular who telephoned her every week to check up on her. It would also appear that Amy is deliberately referencing a feminist text using it as an analogy for her home in the first weeks of bereavement.

Amy: The other person who was so important at that time was Rebecca, my spiritual director. I spent nearly the whole hour with her in tears, but came out refreshed as her outlook was both spiritual and empathetic. I think she was definitely one of my mainstays and still is.

Here Amy identifies a specific individual who is a continuing spiritual and empathetic support.

Int: Sometimes bereavement means being lonely – were you helped in any way to being able to come to terms with being on your own? Are you still being helped?

Amy: I think the thing I really had to learn was how to cope on my own. Initially when I went back to work...and I visited ITU and it was the ward clerk there who was there when James died who said "first time round? Just don't look to the right, walk through slowly...you'll be O.K." But I did look to the right though – I had to. But she watched me and was just there should I not have been able to do it.

Here, Amy recalls the support of a woman in her work place and the quiet evidence of support.

Amy: There were occasions when the tactlessness of people beggared belief...(deletion) ...I could have throttled him.

Here we see Amy's anger at inappropriate comments from a man.

Amy: In winter I leave the hall light on and the front room curtains closed, then it looks as if someone is in when I come home and it doesn't look so empty, cold and unfriendly. I still do this and I expect I always will.

Our informant tells us, here, of her continuing strategy of managing on her own at home.

*Amy: I made a real effort to go out whenever anyone invited me out. I didn't care where I got invited to go. I just went. I still think that was the best thing I ever did – it meant that after six months if I said I couldn't manage it, people knew I would still go out. I was scared of being left totally on my own and I knew if I just went to work and didn't go out I'd never be invited so I really **would** be on my own.*

Amy's reporting what she feels to be an especially coping strategy that works for her and for those who know her. At the same time Amy acknowledges her own anxieties about the potential to become an isolate.

Amy: I think it's not about being lonely..it's just that you are alone. I do have plenty of friends I can visit, who come and visit and stay, so there is company, but you are still alone. You have to cope with everything....putting the bins out...letting the gas servicing people in etc. There's no-one else to do it. You have to whether you like it or not. I can remember an awful thunderstorm one night about a couple of years after James died..it was so close and I hate thunderstorms. I landed up turning the light on as I was so frightened... and that was a time when I really missed James.

First of all, Amy makes a distinction between being lonely and being alone. She speaks of the company of many friends but also identifies the isolation in dealing with the day to day household management tasks. She then goes on to talk about a sense of absence of James.

Amy: The fact that you are alone is difficult when it comes to parties, weddings etc. I was invited to a wedding the February after James died...it was Ayleen's daughter. To be honest I was dreading it.....but in the end it worked out all right. Ayleen is a very thoughtful person and she made sure one of her single friends sat next to me, was on the same table...I also knew a lot of people there which helped enormously and possibly the kindest thing said was by Ayleen's husband – "You're part of our family now" That was a moment when I really had to gulp. One of my church friends, Vera also says her whole family regard me as part of them too... again really kind.

This is the second formal occasion where we see Amy acknowledging her own anxieties and the importance of friends including her. It would seem that these inclusive behaviours militate against Amy's sense of loneliness.

Amy: I flung myself into all sorts of things...I managed two years at university attempting to do a further degree and then leaving when I realised I just wasn't coping. Jo my youngest daughter when I told her told me I wasn't daft...it's just that I didn't have the language. And she was right..I managed a Masters in (deletion) simply because I have the language...but I don't have the language for the degree I was attempting to do...it was disappointing but a sensible move.

Amy speaks of her tactics for widening her horizons and recognises with her daughter's prompting her own limitations and preferences.

*Amy: The house didn't become a home until Josie asked if I'd put up an Eastern European person over on an exchange visit with students. It just made the house **feel** like a point when visitors started to come and stay more and it made the house seem more friendly, more open and more welcoming as it always used to be.*

Amy reminisces on how the house used to be when James was alive and the change that has taken place, which obviously distressed her to some extent. It clearly was very important for her that the house became a home once again and for Amy to be acknowledged as a host in her own right. This would appear to be a significant turning point for Amy.

Int: What sort of support did the church give you?

Amy: I have a lot of church friends...mainly women who still support me. The priest in charge couldn't cope with the bereavement...he's not once been round pastorally, only business wise. Another clergyman called round after James died..."I can manage Saturday either 9 or 9.30 a.m." That was helpful...I wasn't getting up much before 9 a.m. and at the time Carol was staying as well. This was followed by.."so what did James die from?"...another helpful start to a bereavement conversation. I was frankly astonished at the poor pastoral care meted out by the church. Caroline was the only exception.

Amy's reports of the support given to her by the church offer a fairly dismal picture of male parish clergy in her experience. They avoid discussing her bereavement or if they do venture into this territory, they offer limited time and inappropriate conversational gambits. Again, Amy acknowledges the support of women friends.

> *Amy: My colleagues in the hospital team were the other exception – Sam just enfolded me in the biggest bear hug you could possibly ask for which was just lovely. It's been the women in the church who have given the most support…just listening, watching and being there…totally invaluable.*

The other exception with the female member of clergy are Amy's hospital colleagues. She mentions by name the team member who 'enfolded' her in a bear hug and the amount of support she was given by them. However, she reiterates the role women have played in 'listening' and 'being there' as being vital to her.

> *Amy: Our daughters and I sorted out James' belongings in the following August..(deletion) …and I suggested to both of them that we had a memory case for James which they could put anything in that meant a lot to them. It sits on top of a wardrobe, untouched but we all know it's there. With a lot of James' books I gave them to the libraries in Zimbabwe which James used to support…Josie took these. The poetry books I've kept as he loved poetry and so do I. His desk went to Gillian at work and I know he would have liked that too..his computer to Tom and Nancy…again I know James would have approved and that in a way made me feel better. I still have memories of the house next door being emptied and a whole pile of photos being thrown on to a skip and all I could think was "that was someone's life…how can you just dump stuff out like this? Where's the respect?....and I didn't want that to happen to James' belongings.*

Amy opens this passage with reference to 'our daughters'; she seems to do this whenever James is present in her recollections. She goes on to describe their shared engagement with choosing personal mementos of James. The following dialogue describes how Amy acted in accordance with her feelings about things that James would have wished for. She also stipulates her reasons for being so particular about James' belongings by citing her memories of the skip containing someone's whole life that was being disposed of as rubbish.

Int: Are you still being supported by these people?

Amy: Yes I am

Int: Did you find it easier to talk to women or men or both about James' death?

Amy: It was easier to talk to women. A lot of men found the emotional aspect of bereavement difficult to come to terms with…I think they found it awkward and didn't know what to say. Actually, all they needed to do was to listen and just to be there…nothing more. It was only later on that I learned about Shivah, where the bereaved are visited constantly for the first week and where the visitors don't say anything until the bereaved person does and then they listen. How sensible is that?
I can remember Karen's husband saying that when Shivah is over, you don't want another visitor for the next seven years…..at the end of Shivah you are allowed to go out so that you can see the world around you is still going on. That was something I did find difficult..having to go out and return to work and just seeing everyday life going on, where I wanted to scream at them and yell "How can you carry on in this way? Don't you know I need you just to stand still and let me cry when I want to?"

First of all, we have Amy's observations that she found it easier to talk to women and that a lot of men found it awkward and lacked an emotional vocabulary in times of grief. Secondly the Rabbi in Chapter Two talks about the importance of Shivah in Judaic mourning rituals and Amy comments on the sense that these rituals made to her. She also comments on how hard it was to resume her everyday life after James' death. She reports that she carries on working when all she wants is the time and space to grieve.

*Amy: And there were a number of occasions when I did cry. I cried in the bank – the poor lad there went and…you guessed it….a woman who was just lovely. Then there was the time I cried down the phone when I rang the bank and the lady at the other end was just **so** lovely. You remember people like that.*

This episode in the bank marks another formal farewell to James where bank account details must be changed albeit very close to the funeral farewell. It is not surprising to Amy that it is a woman who rescues the situation.

Amy: I can also remember the look of horror on some of the staff's faces when a medical person said "I haven't seen you for ages, Amy, have you been on holiday?" Poor bloke…he was mortified.. but he wasn't to know. That department sent a huge bouquet of flowers as well….really kind.

Amy describes the shock amongst her colleagues when a medical person, unknowingly, draws an incorrect conclusion about her absence. Amy's work community assumed that all members were aware of her recent bereavement and were shocked when this proved not to be the case.

Amy: I went to the transplant service at a local church in the December too – that was so difficult but I just felt I needed to go. James' corneas have enabled two people to be able to see again, so that was a gift I know he would have wanted to give.

Again, Amy acknowledges the importance of complying with James' wishes and we can note that this often involved a gift that James would want to see made.

Amy: It was also difficult sorting out the house…with some of his stuff I had to know it would go to the right home…so as I said previously, the desk went to Gillian and his computer to Tom and Nancy and he would have liked that. And some of his books…about fourteen bags full…went

*out to Zimbabwe to the libraries out there…again he supported that and
would have approved. That was important to me and the recipients
knew and were supportive.*

Amy celebrates giving on James' behalf and the knowledge that those receiving those gifts would value them. We are tempted to suggest that in valuing these gifts they might also be felt to be valuing his life.

*Amy: I find the most difficult thing to contend with are the changes that
have gone on. It almost seems as if you're betraying someone by letting life
go on. Jo has two children – James knew she was expecting Jeremy but
not about Rosie…Jeremy on seeing a photo of James and me asked who my
friend was.. that was really hard… and you still get occasions like that…
again that's where friends are so great…and it's women.*

Amy acknowledges that her greatest challenge is being pulled in two directions. James and Amy clearly both loved their family. For Amy, continuing that love is important and this is jarred when a grand-child wonders who is the man beside his grandmother in the photograph.

WHAT DOES AMY TELL US ABOUT GRIEVING?

Amy offers a pretty precise chronology that includes a range of significant practical arrangements and acknowledges the support of her daughters in coping with these. Amy tells us that death and outside assistance are coupled together, acknowledging the immediate difficulties individuals face following the death of a loved one. We should note that Amy worked in a hospital and hence was familiar with hospital settings; official roles within them and the impact that death has on hospital staff. It is women members of the hospital staff who are particularly recalled by Amy. Unusually, this informant was familiar with procedures at the point of death and able to acknowledge the diversity of belief that goes beyond 'passing on'. She uses the expression 'daft' to describe her own shocked response as well as the formal response 'passed on'.

A SENSE OF SEQUENCE:

We noted earlier that Amy offered a pretty precise chronology, although readers will see that she did not necessarily follow a precise order of events in her re-telling.

She tells us that immediately after James died, social interactions were just a blur, although she found personal engagements where James was absent were the hardest with which to contend. It is interesting to note that Amy was rescued by a woman in the bank, when she displayed her grieving publicly. A visit by an academic from a foreign university prompted Amy to acknowledge an important turning point; that her house was a home and that she was the host.

By involving her daughters in choosing personal mementos of James allowed all three of them to share their personal cherished memories of him. It was also important for Amy that at key points in her journey she was able to feel that she was acting in accordance with what would have been James' wishes.

Amy acknowledges that there were times when grieving hit her unexpectedly, witness the account of her grandchild asking who her 'friend' was. However, she does mention the on-going, reciprocal support she has from a friend when unexpected events like this occur.

A SENSE OF THE PERSONAL:

In the early stages of bereavement, Amy found that a twenty-minute visit was quite long enough. She also comments on the significance of cakes which were brought by the female member of clergy and two men. She mentions Shivah and how Judaic tradition means that the bereaved receives visitors for the first seven days before venturing out into the public sphere and how sensible she feels this is.

She felt that there was a distinction between being lonely and 'alone': in particular the latter when dealing with day to day household management. However, she was impressed by the inclusive behaviour of others which militated against loneliness and the fact that people were happy to 'just listen' and be there with her. Above all she valued the practical support, kindness and compassion she was given.

A SENSE OF GENDER:

We felt that running through Amy's narrative there were some distinctions between some of the men she encountered and most of the women. In particular, she mentions by name, twice as many women as men and how much she valued their support. In contrast to this she comments on the lack of experience of Joshua and the restricted time allowed by another male member of the clergy when visiting her. She felt that her male visitors were inclined to avoid discussion of bereavement and lacked an appropriate vocabulary for encountering and sharing the grief of another. Indeed, one managed a completely tactless comment. In contrast to such behaviour, others, including Anglican clergymen, were able to empathise and offer kindness and compassion.

For Amy, this is not a simple polarisation, but it does bring into sharp contrast the propensity that women have for reaching out to those who are grieving and the struggle that the simple act seems to pose for some men.

7

BARRY'S STORY

Int: What happened after Pauline died? People outside the family who helped during difficult days?

Barry: Well the first thing is Pauline dying was no surprise at all. It had been on the cards for sixteen years. We got by for fourteen of those years and then went down quite suddenly in fact, well fifteen, let's say thirteen of those years, then began to go down quite steeply. Then she could no longer walk more than about twenty yards at a time, so was in a wheelchair.

A CCORDING TO BARRY, his experience of Pauline was that she was quite poorly, but suddenly after thirteen years her health declined and she was no longer mobile and this was characterised by her need for a wheelchair. These points are made as part of Barry organising his narrative.

Barry: Was in hospital three times in five months before she died. (Pause) The second – the penultimate and the last time, I really thought in the ambulance this was going to be the end.

The long pause here and the self-correction lead us to think Barry is thoughtfully organising his narrative. He has taken us to the point where he really thought that Pauline was going to die. Because of what happened in the ambulance Barry was able to gather his thoughts more clearly.

> *Barry: So really, in theory I was prepared, you know, I sort of knew it was going to happen pretty well, although even in that last three and half weeks, you know, there were times of hope, which, um, which didn't come to anything in the end*

Barry continues to thoughtfully organise his narrative, telling us that ultimately his hopes were not going to be realised.

> *Barry: and quite suddenly, they said she was actually to have physio, with a view to sort of getting back and up again.*

Barry lets us know how surprising he found the decision to give Pauline physiotherapy.

> *Barry: She was in bed on oxygen. She'd been on oxygen for nearly two years anyway. She wasn't showing much progress there at all, so I sort of, I suggested, what about physio to see if you can get her up and moving about a bit? and they arranged that and then one day. (Pause) er, um.. What was happening? I was sleeping there overnight, Matthew and Mark both around during the last two weeks of that three and a half weeks and I, what happened? Yeah. (Pause)*

What we are seeing is one start to the story whereby Pauline is in bed on oxygen and another start to the story where Barry proposes physio and then a third start where Barry explains that he was sleeping overnight and both his sons were around. Then Barry confirms to himself that he has recollected just what has happened.

Barry: That's right. It was one morning the physios were coming, so I went off and got some breakfast or came home and got shaved or something like that and came back there and she was sitting, looking very, very exhausted in the chair beside the bed, obviously far more affected by the physical effort that had been made by, as a result of the physio and.. nurses got her into bed and she went to sleep straight away and about an hour later, less than that possibly, a bit vague about that, could have been some hours later, they came along and said, well as you know they do blood gases, tests and then they said, well those tests show that she's not going to live much longer anyway, which was quite surprising at the time cos it wasn't really a shock but it was a bit surprising, you know.

Barry is normally very precise but at this point he says he tells us he is a bit vague about timings, although the key point is that a member of the hospital staff told Barry that his wife was not going to live much longer. Barry says he was surprised and separates that out from being shocked and confirms that it was surprising.

Barry: There hadn't been any <u>marked</u> deterioration in the last week or so except that after this physio session she was completely knocked out and we hardly spoke at all.

Here, Barry gives us his reasons for his surprise at being told Pauline did not have much longer to live.

Barry: At that point I decided that I didn't really want to (pause).. and what was on my mind that in our early years of marriage, several times, Pauline had always been fairly frail and I remember her being frightened she was going to die a couple of times, and, so, I thought I don't want her to possibly risk,(pause).. she was a different person then obviously, but I didn't want to risk the chance of her being frightened and so on, so I said, well I don't really want her to know what's happening, so they just went through the usual procedure, which they do and just gave her a series of injections and so on and she lasted about two and a half days, I think, after that and died very peacefully.

Barry tells us how he wants to protect his wife by not telling her of her imminent death due to what had happened to her in the past. He lets us know that Pauline had always been fairly frail and had been frightened in the past about dying and he did not want her to be frightened now that she actually was dying. He observes that she died very peacefully. The fact that Pauline 'died very peacefully' is an important part of Barry's story.

> *Barry: Matthew and I were just there. I had bought an oxymeter because as far as I could see Ward x was sharing it with Ward xx or something, the oxymeter and so, and so we were watching that all the time and adjusting the oxygen levels and so on, which the nurses weren't too keen on, on the other hand (laughter) they didn't pursue it. They just made sort of oblique remarks, you know, (laughter) you're supposed to know what you're doing and, yes we do actually, we adjust it so that the level goes up to sort of a viable level instead of an unviable level.*

Here Barry tells us that they were able to care for Pauline themselves as they had bought their own oxymeter, due to a shortage of equipment in the hospital, and were capable of using it to test Pauline's oxygen levels. He tells us that the nursing staff was not too keen on this, but that they were not stopped as they had been quite firm in stating that they knew what they were doing. Barry was prepared to confront the power structure around them in order to look after Pauline and here Barry is recalling these awkward moments and they are marked by laughter.

> *Barry: And yes Mark was there, so actually Matthew was there, when she actually died. And he did it just using the oxymeter. He sort of realised she'd been very still for a long time. She used to move about very slightly and that hadn't happened, so he put the oxymeter on and there was no response from it, so he told the nurse, the male nurse there, and he didn't*

*feel up to ringing me and telling me. The male nurse went through the
gentle lead through of course, which of course was quite unnecessary. The
moment he rang, I knew what had happened, and so we packed up.*

Barry again corrects his narrative by saying that it was Matthew who had been
present at Pauline's death and not Mark, and that he had realised she had been
very still for a long while. At this point Matthew used the oxymeter and when
there was no response contacted the nurse because he realised that something
was very wrong. Barry tells us that Matthew had not felt comfortable telling
his father of Pauline's death and that it had been the male nurse who had im-
parted the news to him. Barry says he knew immediately the telephone rang,
what had happened.

Int: Where were you?

*Barry: I was here at the time. Matthew was with her and I'd come home
to get some food or something. I was going to go back to stay overnight
and Matthew was going to stay here. So we packed up everything, which
didn't take very long. He went home on the train because Mathilda was
there by herself with a very troublesome daughter, whom only Matthew
can have much influence. And then I contacted the vicar the next day. I
imagine, not sure. I'm very vague about all sorts of things because in those
days afterwards I did so many silly things.*

Barry had explained why his son could not stay with him and claims to be
very vague on a basis of doing 'silly things'. In actual fact as we shall see, it was
the 'silly things' that he remembers in particular and in great detail.

*Barry: I thought I was all right and technically I wasn't because I went
up on the train to Matthew, bought the ticket at my local station with
a credit card, thank God, and I'd taken a laptop with me. It was the
first train journey for years and years and I took the laptop Matthew had
given me some months before and sort of used it on the train to see what*

I could do with it and got to London, found I had no wallet and I'd put on trousers which looked better than the trousers I'd been wearing, but I realised afterwards, they're the ones with the very short pockets and I keep my wallet in my back pocket there, so it wasn't there.

Barry acknowledges that although he thought he was able to cope immediately after Pauline's death, in actual fact he was not. He tells us how it was that he came to lose his wallet travelling to London, which is an example of Barry not being all right. He realises he needed a fresh pair of trousers to travel, but acknowledges he selected ones with inappropriate pockets.

Barry: So, I got up to get the ticket to a London underground station, found I had about £2.20 in coins and nothing else with me at all, went back to the train station. The train was still there. I wandered up and down, looking under seats, you know, trying to remember where it was and got all the information of where to, you know, they said it'd be searched thoroughly and try locally when you get back. Just had enough money to get a ticket to Matthew's. It was still the middle of the afternoon, so it was fine. I went along to the bank, told them what had happened and she confirmed who I was by asking me what train I caught locally, you know, and she apparently could look up what time. I'd paid for it by credit card luckily and she could look on the credit card record and see, yes I bought it and there was the record that the card has been used ten minutes before. So she gave me a lot of money.

Although Barry says he did 'silly things', he was in actual fact quite organised. He got back to the station, found the train he had travelled on, searched the train for his wallet, talked to a member of the railway staff about losing it and got advice on getting it back. He then went to the bank and was able to provide sufficient detail for the bank to allow him to withdraw cash.

Barry: What happened then? Something really stupid happened again, because the next thing was, I lost a lot of that money, walking back to

Matthew and Mathilda's. Again, probably a pocket thing, but this was something like £150 that was...and so there's been £150 in the wallet and what I was bitterly disappointed about was there was a Marks and Spencer gift card which Matthew had given me for my birthday and that had £60 on it.

Barry, here, is more upset about losing the gift card from his son for £60 than losing £150. We are asked to accept that Barry's greater distress at losing a gift from his son than losing cash is another example of a 'silly thing'. We find this quite understandable and are interested that Barry describes it as a 'silly thing'.

Barry: But things like that went on. I was losing things all over the place for some time. And then addressing all the technicals which the vicar was rather helpful with, although the funeral wasn't for three and a bit weeks, I think.

Given Barry's ability to recall events in fairly minute detail, we wonder about him "losing things all over the place for some time". It is clearly an indication of the distress he felt.

Barry: The memorial gardens are very proud of their one a day, aren't they?

Int: Were there particular people outside your family who helped you over those weeks?

The interviewer is being invited into a shared understanding of a provider. As can be seen the interviewer resists collusion with the interviewee.

Barry: Well everybody was very willing to and so on. I can't think of anyone in particular. If I'd asked for anything, I'd have got it, you know. I didn't feel alone, from that point of view at all. I can imagine many situations where people are not as lucky as I am, who would have been in a very difficult state and so on.

Barry is telling us that he felt privileged with all the support he got. He is imagining others in a worse situation than himself. We speculate that what he is doing here is alleviating what must be a very distressing situation, by suggesting others are in far more difficult places than himself.

Int: Which bits did the vicar do?

Barry: The minister had already arranged a funeral for a neighbour over the road. It seemed natural to come to them and that's what we did anyway and they did a lot of guidance as to the memorial gardens. I'd never been there actually and so they sort of, were a point of reference all along, from that point of view. I mean there were lots of other technical points, of course, about winding up. Although there wasn't much to do initially was there cos I, as the survivor, most of it clicked in automatically in fact and it was only the will which was later anyway.

Barry finds it natural to use the minister he knows, rather than somebody else. As will become apparent later in the transcript, Barry also felt it was right to ask an Anglican minister to conduct the service. Barry has shifted away from reflections on the funeral to more practical details.

Barry: There was the technical, changing accounts for example from joint account. Well the bank did that automatically, but other things. We were jointly insured for the car and things like that and for house insurance possibly, I'm not sure about that. But I'm well able to deal with that sort of thing. It doesn't worry me at all.

Barry gives us the specifics of the changes that are required by banks and insurance companies and affirms his confidence in this area. We can note that

Barry spends considerably more time talking about banking and insurance than he does about funeral arrangements.

> *Int: What about planning the funeral? Did the minister say you need to do this, this and this?*

> *Barry: I'm not sure the minister did. I just don't remember that particular at all.*

> *Int: A consultant you could just go and ask?*

> *Barry: Yeah, well the minister is an acquaintance anyway, so it was, and as I said, the minister helped with a neighbour.*

The interviewer has two further attempts to engage Barry in a dialogue about funeral arrangements, but Barry will not be drawn at all about planning Pauline's funeral.

> *Int: You knew the minister helped another family?*

This is the third time the interviewer has attempted to draw Barry on funeral arrangements.

> *Barry: Oh yeah, well I knew from conversations the minister has regularly done other funerals and so on. The minister took another neighbour's funeral.*

Again, Barry deflects questions about funeral arrangements on to others. We speculate that he may find these too difficult to talk about.

> *Int: Did you find people like Ted and Janet helpful?*

Barry: Yeah, well as I said, they would do anything I asked them to do and so on.

Int: What sort of things would they do?

The interviewer asks about Barry's local friends and Barry indicates how generous they were with their offers of help. At this point the interviewer nudges Barry towards providing more detail.

Barry: I can't remember particularly. This is three and a quarter years ago and I'm not sure they did much at all. It was just the minister and me and Mark obviously was very closely involved in that. He was the one who went over to the memorial gardens and looked around there. It may have been twice we went, I'm not sure about that. Matthew wasn't around very much and so on. He'd been up when Pauline was in the last weeks and so on.

This sequence of the interview suggests that this period in Barry's life must have been painful (the way Barry spoke, timbre, pace of utterance, suggests a painful recollection). Barry goes on to identify, unprompted, those who were helpful to him. We can note that he identifies an Anglican minister and his sons as memorably helpful. He has also linked the last weeks of his wife's life with her death.

Barry: If you mean, did anybody say "Come down" and sort of, so you're not by yourself, nothing like that happened at all actually. But I went up to Matthew's very soon, that was anywhere, which financially was a disaster.

Barry then moves on to rephrase the question towards who cared for him. He named a son and refers back to an episode he cited earlier as evidence of "silly" behaviour.

Int: Did Janet organise the flowers?

Barry: Yes, I think she probably did in the end. That's right, that was some weeks later, wasn't it? That was right at the end. That's right we went over to that place in the suburbs. Yes, I'd forgotten that one.

Int: Did neighbours call in?

Barry: No idea. But I know them all so well anyway and so they might have done. I got lots of cards and people came in. I'm sure they came in and sort of knocked at the door and sort of said things and perhaps they came in. But I've no memory of that in particular, at all.

The interviewer moves from a question about a specific neighbour to a more general question. Barry's answer again suggests that the experience was a blur to him although he is confident that his neighbours were respectful and kind.

Int: Were you helped in any way with coming to terms with being on your own?

Barry: Well you have to say by whom and in what circumstances. I don't know. I mean I'm quite a self-sufficient person in any case. And as I say I never got desperately lonely or anything like that, there was always far too much to do in any case and then I spent a couple of weeks, it seemed to me, just writing letters interminably to lots of people. Repeating myself, writing them by hand usually which is something I don't normally do.

When asked about loneliness Barry responds in terms of his own self-sufficiency and of generic tasks associated with Pauline's death.

Int: What about later on, say a year or so later?

Barry: I don't think I can think of – I mean this house is a blessing in a way because there's always so much to be done to it that I spend all my time thinking what next, you know. One of the things I found hard (pause) I sort of consoled myself, I'd always got the arts to take up my time. Pauline and I went to lots of concerts and theatres, operas and so on and I wanted to go with someone and I promoted the idea of operas to some neighbours. I knew Sandra was interested in opera in particular. And in the end, I actually psyched myself up to go into the cinema by myself, which was the first time since I was about 18, I suppose, just before I went to the R.A.F., and that was actually quite difficult. I went down to the Riverside and saw a Woody Allen film called Jasmine, I think, which everybody said was very good. It was a little bit on the miserable side, to put it mildly, it was about a demented woman, basically and I very nearly walked out after about 10, 15 minutes, and I thought, I don't like this. I didn't like being there by myself and on the other hand I'm very keen on money and I thought I'm not going to waste money like that, so I stayed to the bitter end. And once, I'd done that, I wasn't too bad after that and I've been to the cinema a few times. Been to a couple of operas, been to several concerts at College Hall, the University ones and so on. So, I've got over that. That's fine now. Janet persuaded Ted to go with me to see a Shakespeare Coriolanus, on one of these cinema transmission things. He hates real theatre anyway. He says he prefers the words and the poetry and of course, as luck would have it, it was a miserable thing and I didn't like it any more than he did really. So, it reinforced all his prejudices against going to the theatre anyway.

Barry reiterates that he had plenty of things to keep him occupied, particularly in the house. He then deviates a bit by talking about the times that he and Pauline went to performances and how much he initially missed attending them with her. In order to rectify this, he decided to try going to a cinema on his own. He describes himself as 'psyching himself up' in order to go and talks about how difficult it was, particularly as it was not a very happy film. However, this experience did give Barry the confidence to go out on his own to the arts. Then he reports going to another miserable production with a neighbour. Positive experiences are generic for Barry and miserable experiences appear to be specific. So, he remembers particular miserable experiences but treats all the positive ones as general.

Int: Are you able to talk about the sort of support the church gave or didn't give you?

Barry: Well the minister was the only church contact I had anyway so that was perfect, you know. I mean I'm not an Anglican. Pauline was, sort of. Actually, the last time she went into the hospital, there was yet another of these forms to fill in, as if she'd never been there before, you know and I said, "Are you still an Anglican?" and she said, "Of course." A bit like Andrew Motion, used to be Poet Laureate, and he said he has no Christian faith but really enjoys hymns and things like that. There's a bit of that in me, I think. So, I think the Anglican service is just like the Anglican marriage service. I think it's splendid. It's not extreme in any stupid way and people can make of it what they want, in fact.

Although Barry's wife took her Anglican faith as given and he appreciated the hymns and the liturgy, it was the contact with the Anglican minister that was 'perfect' and the service was comparable to the Anglican marriage service in that it was 'splendid'. Barry makes the comment that with Anglican services people are able to take from them what they specifically want.

Int: Is there anything else you want to add or talk about?

Barry: One of the things I thought might come up and I've not really mentioned to anybody unless they've sort of guessed it from me, but I was always deeply embarrassed about deaths and talking about death and anybody who was bereaved, I was very embarrassed to think, I don't want to say anything that's going to upset them, which probably upset them

more than saying anything, as I've realised since. So I made a point actu-
ally of sort of indicating that it's perfectly all right to talk about Pauline
if they want to, you know. We'll be having a joke, I'll say, "Pauline did
you hear what he's saying, what do you..Oh Pauline agrees with you" I
do things like that quite deliberately and just to sort of free it up. I can't
think it's had any effect whatsoever, actually cos nobody's said. But they
do know that Pauline isn't off limits and so on, in case they were as naïve
and innocent and silly as I was about it all that time and so on.

Barry begins to talk about the embarrassment of grief and then indicates his
own strategy for putting others at their ease was to engage in an imaginary,
affectionate exchange with Pauline to enable others to also speak of her. He
reviews his own reactions to bereaved people in the light of his own bereavement. He is keen to put others at their ease and recognises that people need
to be given permission to talk about the deceased with the bereaved because
he now understands how others might have felt.

Int: Did anybody really not want to talk about it?

Barry: Not that I know. All my friends are either quite close or they don't
exist at all, in fact. No, I can imagine people like that. I've got into meet-
ings, like the ones on the last Sundays and so on. They wouldn't know
whether I was…The only person I ever talked to about it funnily enough
was one of those last Sundays, it was he was a head teacher of somewhere,
going a long way back and his wife had died suddenly and I remember
him bringing up the subject and said my wife's died and that was really,
really hard, he said. Now that happened about a year before, I think and
so on and he was able to talk about it. But I think she died at a younger
age than Pauline had in fact. I'm not quite sure about that. I think I
imagine bereavement is like the same for everybody and completely differ-
ent for everybody. Generalising is a bit of a dangerous pattern, I should
think.

First of all, Barry acknowledges a continuing struggle in talking about death and bereavement. He then goes on to make what we regard as a very telling observation, that bereavement is the same for everybody and completely different for everybody. Because of this, Barry cautions against generalising.

Int: Did anybody tell you time is a great healer?

Barry: No. I might have laughed in their face. Well are you opposed to evil in favour of good, you know. No, nobody came out with anything as trite as that. And the other thing, nobody, see one of my thoughts is…I thought once, if anybody said, you know, you're going to get over this, or anything on those lines, it'll all sort of fade away. I'm quite prepared to take them on and say, "I don't want it to fade away" you know, I don't want my feelings to be somehow degraded, which would be completely wrong. But it won't happen.

Here the interviewer is testing a cliché which Barry rejects quite forcibly and this allows him to go on to say that he does not want his memories to be dulled and through this for his feelings about Pauline to be eroded.

Int: Initially did you feel that it was something that enveloped you totally after Pauline died? Do you still feel that now?

Barry: Yes, yes, that's not quite the word I'd use. Like a little black cloud over you, but yeah. No, I'd agree with that, yeah. I mean one of the things was I didn't cry and at one stage I thought I ought to cry and I actually set out to make myself cry and failed totally. But what did happen, after quite some weeks, it would sort of come over me and I would actually physically shake in some way. Not like making myself do that but it was an involuntary action and I was just sort of shaking and I just wonder if that was an equivalent of a crying episode and so on.

Barry agrees with the interviewer that his grief was something that enveloped him and he describes it as a 'little black cloud over you'. He then goes on to talk about his inability to cry, as though crying was an expectation of a grieving person. However, he finds an equivalent for himself in his later physical responses to memories of Pauline.

Int: A physical reaction?

Barry: Yeah, that's right and it just sort of came on to me, you know. I'd think of something. You know, I'd see Pauline's clothes in the wardrobe, something like that you know, I'd be there.

Int: It's the little things

Barry: Yeah, you suddenly realise, God this is so big, what's happened to me. You know, I did eventually get rid of all Pauline's clothes. No I didn't, I've got some in the wardrobe that I wouldn't get rid of.

Barry confirms his response to memories of Pauline is a physical response, for example when he finds items of Pauline's clothing. This reminiscence leads him to reflect on the special items he has kept in remembrance of her.

Barry: Yeah, that was probably the hardest thing because that went on for months in fact. Actually Annette's sister in law, that's Euan's sister, she's a professional concert pianist, but she still needs money because her husband has got the same lung disease as Pauline had. He's 80 now. Nearly all Pauline's clothes fitted her very well, so again, this embarrassment thing. Annette said, "Would you like the idea of someone else wearing Pauline's clothes?" and I said, "Yeah, I don't have any trouble with that, at all." I've kept the ones that mean so much to me. The other ones, I'm pleased they can be used for something. Don't know whether it's sentimentality but down in the basement there's a trunk......and it's got all Mark's and

Matthew's toys from when they were little......I couldn't get rid of it, neither of us could in fact.

Barry goes on to reminisce about her clothes and this then takes him to remembrances of his children's childhoods.

Int: It's as though you're sort of maintaining contact with the person.

Barry: Yeah, that's a contact from a very happy time of life in fact. I know exactly when the happiest time of my life was. It was Matthew was – no Mark was one and my mother who'd been making our life hell for several years and had done right up till then, went off to London, school holidays, second week of the summer holidays, so September so far away, doesn't count and Mark could walk about and run and we had a paddling pool in the back garden in Hightown Avenue and the weather was perfect for a week.

Int: A very strong family time. Family was your real happiness in life.

Barry: It was just the three of us in fact. We kept out Pauline's family, who were nothing like my mother, who was trouble and so on that was going to come. No it was just the three of us and all pressures were off, for just one week, you know. There was no school around. We weren't going anywhere. Nobody was coming to us. It was just us and this delightful one year old....six months he'd been an absolute swine and then he changed dramatically.

Barry reminisces about his happiest time with Pauline and his family.

Int: Did you find it easier to talk to women or men about Pauline's death?

Barry: Oh it would be women, I think. Undoubtedly, yeah

Int: Why is that?

Barry: Don't know. I find women much more interesting to talk to than men in most cases anyway. Men talk is all about politics or unimportant things. I talk to women about medical conditions at quite an alarming rate of detail at times, which first takes them aback and then they're quite pleased.

Int: Why do you think that is?

Barry: I never thought about why it is. I know it's true for me anyway. I think I've come to the conclusion that women are much more valuable members of humanity than most men are.

Int: Your well being – being able to talk about how you are>

Barry: Yeah, I've never spoken really. I mean men will talk about health but they'll only exchange symptoms really and so on. My symptoms are bigger than yours. It doesn't get that much more technical with women actually but I feel that the conversation is more useful and seems to mean something good. I may be just imagining things.

Barry affirms he finds it easier to talk to women about Pauline's death. First of all, women are more interesting to talk to, more tolerant of his discussion of medical detail and more valuable members of humanity than most men are. Secondly, he feels that conversation with women is beneficial. He sees men, on the other hand, as competitive and only willing to discuss politics or themselves.

Int: Does empathy play into that?

Barry: Well I think it must do to some extent.

Int: Women are more empathetic

Barry: Oh yeah. Well more openly.

In conclusion, he confirms that women are more openly empathetic than men.

WHAT DOES BARRY TELL US ABOUT GRIEVING?

CLARITY AS A PRECURSOR TO BEREAVEMENT

First of all, there is a careful attempt to produce a sequence of events. Barry goes to some lengths to organise his narrative in chronological order. Although Barry is normally very precise in this interview, he has three attempts at beginning his narrative, struggling to sequence the events. He shows himself to be shocked and surprised at being told that his wife was not going to live much longer, even though at the beginning of the interview he says that her death had been on the cards for thirteen years. Barry recalls feeling very protective over his wife who had been frightened about dying in the past and he did not want her to be frightened when moving towards her death. Barry sounded grateful that she had had a 'peaceful death'.

Barry is particularly clear about the role of an oxymeter in Pauline's death. The family brought in their own oxymeter because a shortage of equipment at the hospital was impacting on their loved one's dying days. The family used the oxymeter to monitor and adjust Pauline's oxygen supply regardless of the presence of hospital staff. Their private confidence, in contrast to professional competence, is marked by a kind of knowing laughter. It was monitoring the oxymeter that led one of Barry's sons to realise that something was very wrong and to call for a nurse, who in turn contacted Barry to tell him that his wife had died.

VAGUENESS AS A CONSEQUENCE OF BEREAVEMENT

When trying to recall the events immediately following Pauline's death, Barry becomes quite vague. He talks about doing 'silly things' in particular mislaying his wallet and quite a large sum of cash. He says that his bank was very helpful with these 'silly things'. He goes on to say that he thought it was a silly thing to value a gift voucher from his son more than the cash he had lost. The way this story was told made it clear how much he valued his son's gift. Barry was very vague about funeral arrangements and did not particularly want to talk about them. He was vague about his neighbours' involvement after his wife's death and although he reports it as 'all a blur' it seems they were respectful and kind. In contrast to this vagueness, Barry was particularly precise about some miserable experiences following early attempts to engage with the wider world although he treated positive experiences in a more general way.

ANGLICAN MINISTRY

Barry tells us that he found it natural to approach an Anglican minister he knew and that it felt right to ask this minister because of preceding faith conversations he had had with his wife. He tells us that the Anglican minister was perfect and that the service was splendid. He remarks that he thinks people are able to take from Anglican arrangements what they specifically want.

REFLECTIONS ON PERSONAL GRIEF

Barry acknowledges that prior to being bereaved himself, he felt a sense of embarrassment when talking with other bereaved people. However, since Pauline's death he is now keen to put others at their ease, recognising that people need to be given permission to talk about the deceased with the bereaved and that he now understands how others might have felt. However, he does talk about his continuing struggle in talking about death and bereavement. Barry rejects clichés about death and goes on to say that he does not want his memories to be dulled or his feelings about Pauline eroded. In a poetic moment, he describes grief as a 'little black cloud' over you. In some ways, it seems as though he struggles with the idea of crying being equated with grief, although he later found an equivalent in his physical responses to things that reminded him of Pauline. Indeed, memories about Pauline's clothing and special items kept in remembrance of her were linked by Barry to family mementos of his children's childhood.

Barry shared, what was to us, a very telling observation about bereavement. He said that he thought that bereavement is the same for everybody and completely different for everybody. He cautioned us against trying to generalise about bereavement and grief.

REFLECTION ON GENDER

When reflecting on his experience of bereavement, Barry talked quite a lot about the differences between men and women. He affirmed that he found it easier to talk to women as he felt they were more interesting and beneficial to talk to and more tolerant of discussion of medical detail, compared with men whom he felt were competitive and tended to discuss politics and themselves. He went on to say that he felt women were actually more valuable members of humanity than men. Women are, he said, more openly empathetic than men.

SOME PERSONAL DISCURSIVE FEATURES

Barry describes things as 'technical' on six occasions. These are usually related to financial matters such as banking and insurance, but there are two exceptions to this. The first of these is when he speaks of his personal, emotional well-being where he tells us he thought he was 'technically' all right, although he wasn't, and the second of these is when he speaks of 'technical' conversations, those that are medically detailed.

Barry uses the phrase 'and so on' sixteen times in the course of our interview. Not all the uses are identical and we can describe the occurrences as mostly centred on emotionally difficult areas (six times). He uses the expression as an umbrella for relevant medical details sometimes actual, at another time conversational (three times). In describing his social life, he uses 'and so on' to cover similar events to those he had been talking about (three times). He uses it to cover the wide variety of help he was offered after bereavement (two times). He uses it once as an extension of how busy his family are and once as a 'filler' to maintain his conversational flow.

From this analysis of usage, it is apparent that he elides personal and emotional difficulties which occur with surprising frequency during the interview. The next most elided areas are medical details, financial matters and the kinds of events Barry attends.

8

SAUL'S STORY

INTERVIEW WITH SAUL WITH EMBEDDED COMMENTARY.

Int: I wonder if you could talk your way through what happened after Esther died, especially those people outside the family who helped most during those difficult days.

Saul: Yes. Well in many respects there was a sense of relief because we knew that she had been suffering a lot and in fact had been in a coma for several days and when eventually she died on the Sunday morning as I say there is considerable relief. Diana was with her at the end, she'd stayed overnight in the hospital in the ward that Esther was in and, she was, she was very, very stoic very – (Pause) what shall I say very real, very realistic in her approach to what had happened. And Lester and I got down to the hospital approximately twenty minutes after Esther had died.

THE INTERVIEWER ASKS Saul to recall events following Esther's death with a focus on those outside the family. At this point Saul gives a detailed account of exactly what had happened when his wife died. He starts by reflecting on the relief that her suffering was over. He comments on how stoic, yet realistic Diana (his daughter – field notes) was about Esther's death. Saul places an emphasis on Diana's stoicism but then, thinking aloud, modifies this to realism. It is as if Saul recognises that Diana was a 'rock' for him at this difficult time. We can see Saul offering an initial chronology within which he recognises the importance of family members.

Saul: During the last few days, many people had visited Esther and many people had visited me here at home and I had tremendous support from close friends, from family of course, but, one very surprising element in that, was my niece or Esther's niece who turned up trumps and was very supportive of me, emotionally, and came in, she doesn't live that far away, came in and called on us quite, quite frequently.

Saul then talks about the generalised others who helped him, but mentions specifically Esther's niece who visited regularly and supported him emotionally.

Saul: The support from both churches from St. Basil's and from the local parish Church was tremendous and, after Esther's death I was surrounded by good friends, good, wonderful members, members of my family and good neighbours. I could not have asked for more.

Saul mentions at this stage, the support he had from the church he attended and the one that his wife attended (taken from field notes). He does not at this stage specify exactly what support he received but he is very complimentary about this support. He says how widely distributed his support network was and identifies the church, good friends, members of his family and neighbours.

Saul: My own feelings at the time were, oh, ones of devastation I suppose. I've covered the relief feeling but, there was also a feeling of, not exactly regret, but a feeling that I was - (Pause) trying to escape from something which I knew I shouldn't escape from. Facing up to grief I found to be very, very taxing. I don't think you can ignore grief, I don't think that you should if you do try to ignore grief then you, you let down the one you have lost. You betray them in a way I feel.

Saul emphasises that he found facing up to grief very taxing and very hard. He also states that ignoring grief, on the other hand, is akin to betrayal of the deceased and that he could not do this. His loyalty to Esther is very apparent.

Saul: So you've got to face up to grief and you've got to learn to live with it, and you've got to learn that it is part of life, for a very, very large proportion of the population in any case. You're never, you're never alone in this, never and it's... That in its way is a comfort and although we can argue that individually cases are different of course, one from another and people take bereavement differently, it's one of the facts of life and you've got to learn to cope. That's how I felt, that's how I've felt since.

Saul summarises where he has got to in his narrative and then he goes on to share his belief that it happens to everybody and you have to face up to it. Saul feels that there are three things you have to learn about grief: learning to live with it, learning that it is part of life and learning to cope with bereavement. On the other hand, he acknowledges that no one is alone in this and that that in itself is a comfort. When Saul emphasises you are never alone, he is referring to God never leaving you (field notes).

Saul: I am as I have said many times before to people, a very easy weeper, I cried, cried and cried. Still do from time to time. But I don't regret crying and no one's ever, no one has ever reprimanded me for it, they've never said, pull yourself together Saul for heaven's sake, but in a way, I think, I have every justification of doing so. But as I say people have been extremely kind.

Here Saul is sharing his emotional outpouring with the interviewer, declaring that he has every justification for crying. It is as if Saul is not ashamed of crying, but feels as if others may not quite approve using the phrase 'no one has ever reprimanded me for it' and he needs to justify himself. We find the use of a verb that is as strong as 'reprimanded' gives us pause for reflection. However, it is not incumbent upon him to justify himself because as Saul says, people were extremely kind to him.

Int: Thank you. Can you remember what those people who supported you most said, or did that made that special difference? Was it empathy or sympathy enabling you to talk about your grief or was it practical support, and are you still being supported by those people?

Saul: I still am being supported by those people yes.

(Interrupted by door bell and neighbour calling)

Prior to this interruption the interviewer prompted Saul to provide more detail about the kind of support he received.

Saul: Sorry about that.

Int: That's O.K.

Saul: There's one very, very good neighbour and that's a typical example of someone who looks after me frankly. Practical help – the people who have helped me through the difficult time, taking the dog for a walk, mercifully I haven't needed people to do shopping for me because I've been able to do that myself. One of the very pointed, not pointed, very strong bits of help that we had was from the people who Diana works, who, without hesitation acknowledged her compassionate leave up to Esther's death and for several weeks after, which I think was extremely good. I've now lost my train of thought.

Saul uses the interruption prompted by a neighbour's visit, as an example of the kind of caring support he receives from neighbours. He then goes on to more practical details of how compassionate Diana's employers were, after which he loses his train of thought.

Int: Can you remember what those people who supported you most said or did that made that special difference?

Saul: The most important thing that they said was, remember what Esther was like. Esther was a very practical, no nonsense person, who although she didn't lack human sympathy or empathy as far as that goes, she, she was a roll up your sleeves, let's get on with, kind of person. And that did me good. And the people who helped me most I think, during her illness and after her death were the people who said, you know, remember what she was like, what she was really like and the implication was, and it was a very good one. The implication was don't dwell on your own feelings so much as your good memories of her.

The interviewer prompts Saul and Saul takes the opportunity to talk about Esther. He describes her as a very practical person. In being prompted to remember her as 'how she was' he feels 'does him good'. He goes on to infer that in being 'practical' and remembering the deceased the way they were has enabled him to cope with his grief. Again he implies that dwelling on your own grief is unacceptable and it is preferable to recall the happy memories of Esther.

Saul: Mentally, mentally I'm still waiting for her to come home, cos she went places on her own. She travelled abroad on her own, literally months before she, she became ill and this was part of our, part of the, the pattern of our marriage, and that we, we let one another do what we felt the other needed or wanted to do. So, I am not unused to her not being around because she was away for two weeks at one stage way back when the children were younger. She was abroad visiting her sister for something like six weeks. She would go off to conferences to do with embroidery, conferences to do with patchwork, church work, she used to go on retreat once a year, always quite regularly to the Collum valley. And as far as I was concerned this was fine. But she was also reciprocal in the sense that she would let me go to Europe with my group of friends that I used to go with, and visit my friend for a couple of nights no problem. So, the people who helped me most were those who, reminded me that I should remind myself of the kind of wife I had. Rather than dwell upon my own sadness and I think that was very, very supportive. I mean name wise, the chaplains at the hospital, Hester, Wilma and Nell in the neighbouring parish. People who visited her and visited me in a very normal, how shall I say, pragmatic kind of way.

Saul remembers some of the happy memories he had of Esther, but still admits he is waiting for her to come home. He talks about her travelling and the reciprocal arrangements they had, but then goes on to reiterate that he is remembering what his wife was like and the happy times they had together. For the second time, he reminds himself to think about these happy times rather than dwell on his own sadness. He then goes on to identify particular people who have helped him, who share his faith and are mostly women.

Int: You almost answered, being bereaved can mean loneliness, were you helped in any way to be able to come to terms with being on your own?

Saul: Yes, I mean I'm fortunate in having Diana with me of course. But I'm also fortunate in that I have several people who are my friends whom I visit and who visit me. I've also got my lovely dog, who's laid aside at the moment unfortunately. But although there's a tremendous hole, void in my life, the rest of my life is still there, which I enjoy and which I thank God for every day. And without sounding too religious about it, that's my, my calling in life is to serve Him every day and...We have a wonderful phrase we would remind one another, especially when things were difficult but also when things were lovely. 'We're in God's hands, and always have been'. And that meant so much, so much, still does.

Saul acknowledges that there is a great void in his life, but also acknowledges that he is not exactly 'lonely' as he has his daughter living with him and friends whom he visits and who visit him. He also emphasises that God and his faith are very important in his life and that because he has this belief, he is never lonely. He goes on to remember the saying he and Esther would use whether times were difficult or lovely and emphasises how much this meant and still means to him.

Int: Esther had a religious funeral – what sort of support did the church give to you?

Saul: The support that the church gave me and gave her towards the end, was the kind of support that we've always had. People, people didn't just do what they had always done, they did it, they did it in more depth and with more feeling and with more frequency. But we had communion here, at home, when Esther couldn't get out, we had visits here, we also had people praying for us, we knew that - in both congregations.

Here Saul mostly talks about what the congregations did for him and for Esther.

Int: William came round?

Saul: William came here, another minister came, Nell came here, Hester came here, Joel came here.

Saul answers the interviewer by providing a list of the ministers who came round and supported both him and Esther.

Int: Did Joshua come?

Saul: No. No Joshua did not come here, but he saw me many times either at church or when I was, funnily enough, when I was out walking the dog on the common. And talked about the illness and about the bereavement and reassured me that he and his family were thinking of us, Diana and myself, after Esther's death. Yeah, I mean I think it was a case as far as the parish, of this parish, is concerned was that, he had dedicated as it were the, the pastoral responsibility to William and William fulfilled that as indeed so did another minister (woman – field notes). I have no complaint whatsoever about the way in which the church supported me and Diana. The only difference between, between Diana and myself is that the contacts were probably made electronically by Diana and not by, not by me. I used other means like the telephone, and, and personal visits and meetings. But I think Diana was in touch with, with William and others at St. Basil's by e-mail quite a lot.

The interviewer prompts Saul by referring to a named minister. Saul responds that although that particular minister did not visit, they met frequently, when Saul was walking his dog or at church. Saul knew that he and his family were being thought of by the minister. Saul goes on to explain that he understood that William had been identified as supporting him and his family pastorally. When Saul introduces the idea of 'complaining' into the conversation, he does so only in order to dismiss it. He then refers to generational differences in communication in the church. (written compared with spoken)

Int: Sometimes that can be quite therapeutic, you haven't got to face a person and people feel comfortable in dealing with that. Are you still being supported by those people?

Saul: Yeah, I, I mean I know they're there. I mean my neighbours around here are marvellous. They are really, really marvellous. Of course, we've always been close to our neighbours, we've always not only just chatted to them, but, you know, have been quite happy to go in one another's houses and you know I mean, (deletion), putting one another's bins out when they're on holiday and all this sort of thing you know. But I have spent

*hours with that lady who called just now – I have spent hours over there
with them, talking, weeping, oh, just sitting. They've been marvellous.*

Saul derives help and solace from his neighbours who he reports as a close
community and singles out one couple as having been 'marvellous' because
of the space that they gave him and allowed him just to 'be'. The space that
he was given and was able to share comfortably, was physical, temporal and
emotional.

*Int: Thank you. Did you find it easier to talk to women or men about
Esther's death?*

Saul: No (laughs)

Int: No you didn't find it easy or yes?

*Saul: Frankly I mean this may sound a bit precocious but frankly I've
never even thought of it. I suppose in a way, women tend to be more –
oh, I don't know – it's Mothering Sunday on Sunday – you know what
I mean. They tend (Pause), but I have come across some very tender
hearted lovely men, and not only now but you know, throughout my life,
who I have felt that I could unload to and unburden to in times of difficulty. My own father in law was wonderful, Esther's dad was wonderful.
But, no, not really. I wouldn't differentiate really.*

The interviewer asks Saul if there were any differences between men and
women in being able to converse with them. Saul gets half way through a
statement about how he perceives women but does not finish his sentence.
It is implicit so far that he perceives women as usually more caring. We say
this because he goes on to remark that he has found some men very 'tender
hearted' and able to share burdens with them in times of difficulty. The
phrasing here leads us to believe that he would find that true in general of the
women in his life. As a result of his reflection he does not think there is any

difference, although we note he seems to speak of women in general, and men in particular.

Int: Anything else?

Saul: I'll tell you one, let me. I wouldn't, I'll tell you why I wouldn't differentiate. One of the closest people emotionally to me is my own son, although Florence is also very close emotionally. Diana is a little more distant because Diana is more as I use the word, stoic. Diana is more stoic in her attitude towards life and of course she's single and has in her own words chosen her own lifestyle, therefore views life differently. But that's not the main reason. I mean all I'm saying is that I have never really noticed much difference in, you know, between the sexes with regard to whom I can unburden.

Int: Thank you very much

A fairly standard prompt at the end of the interview leads Saul to attempt further clarification of his views on gender difference illustrating his view by drawing on his own family. Saul does not define gender differences, but instead draws on gender similarities in emotional proximity and in recognising whom he trusts and will allow him to unburden himself. As we reach the end of the interview with Saul, we believe that alongside our prompted reflection on gender, we find an emphasis on Saul's account on unburdening.

WHAT DOES SAUL TELL US ABOUT GRIEVING?

A SENSE OF CHRONOLOGY:
Saul begins by acknowledging a sense of relief that Esther was no longer suffering. This is rapidly followed by a description of one of his daughters, who we have seen as a 'rock' for him in this difficult time, and then with chronological detail. He prioritises reference to family members and

then goes on to speak of the support he received from local churches. At this stage, Saul does not provide any detail of the kind of support he received, although he is very complimentary about it and the range of people involved. Following on from this, Saul goes on to talk about his own feelings.

"FACING UP TO GRIEF":

Saul describes his struggle to come to terms with a mixture of devastation and relief as 'very, very taxing'. Here 'taxing' was a carefully selected description. He says that he does not think it is possible to ignore grief and that if you try to ignore it you let down, betray, the one you have lost. He goes on to identify four lessons the bereaved need to learn. The first of these is that you have to face up to grief; the second is that you have got to learn to live with it; the third is that it is a part of life for nearly everybody and the fourth is that you have got to learn to cope with it. He asserts that these are things he felt at the time and that he still feels today. He goes on to say that we can see grief individually but at the same time it is a fact of life. However, he acknowledges that he is a very easy weeper and that he cried and cried and still does. While being candid about his tears, he also introduces the idea that he might be reprimanded for them but feels he is justified in his tears. He also notes he does not have to justify them, because people were extremely kind to him and did not require his justification. When asked he is quick to point out that he had lots of support.

In discussing his own grief Saul says three times, in quick succession, that it is better to dwell on his good memories of Esther rather than on his own grief, which he said he found very helpful and supportive. Firstly, Saul says it did him good to be encouraged to remember what she was like and secondly, he identifies an implication to be that he should not dwell on his own feelings so much as his good memories of Esther. At the conclusion of this interview Saul places a particular emphasis on unburdening himself and we discuss this further below.

IDENTIFYING A SUPPORTIVE COMMUNITY:

When asked about what supporters did or said, Saul confirms he is still being supported and as if in confirmation, his doorbell rings and a supportive neighbour calls by. This gives Saul the opportunity to talk about people who help, targeting practical help. The interviewer prompts again about what was special about what helpers said or did. Saul responds by referring immediately to advice he was given to remember Esther as she was and Saul reminds himself of the happy memories he has of her. Saul recalls support from the chaplains at the hospital where Esther died and ministers in his neighbouring parish. He mentions four women and one man. The interviewer then prompts about coming to terms with being on his own. He acknowledges a void in his life but goes on to thank God for every day, reminding himself of a phrase he and his wife shared: "We're in God's hands and always have been." He emphasises that his faith is very important in his life and that because of his belief he is never lonely.

When asked if he was still receiving support from the church, he replies by saying he is aware they are there, but acknowledges that they do not come round so much.

He tells us that his neighbours are marvellous, including a couple who found the time to give him physical and emotional support when he needed it. He acknowledges support from neighbours, from the church but particularly from his family.

SUPPORT FROM THE CHURCH:

When the interviewer asks about the sort of support the church gave, Saul says people 'did what they always did' but with greater depth, feeling and frequency. In terms of the clergy, he mentions two men and three women. When asked about a specific minister he reports seeing him while walking his dog. In discussing the support that he and his daughter received, he makes a distinction on generational difficulties in written communication for a younger generation and spoken for an older generation. Saul also introduces the idea of complaining into the conversation but he does so only to dismiss it.

REFLECTIONS ON GENDER:

When asked directly whether he found it easier to talk to women or men about Esther's death, he says he has never thought of it. He starts by alluding to the caring role that women take but quickly modifies this by identifying some tender hearted, lovely men who had been in his life, and therefore says he is unable to differentiate between them. In this discussion, he speaks of women in general and men in particular. We note that when discussing the clergy, he makes particular reference to more women than men. In response to a fairly standard prompt at the end of the interview, Saul provides further clarification of his views on gender differences in relation to grief. He illustrates this by drawing on examples from his own family and finds similarities between men and women in emotional proximity and whom he trusts sufficiently and to whom he is willing to unburden himself.

SOME PERSONAL DISCURSIVE FEATURES:

During his interview Saul used repetitions (very, very/quite, quite/really, really). Sometimes he uses repetition to create a space in which he can select the exact word he is searching for. He does this when describing people and the help they gave him. He also uses repetition for emphasis describing a population at large and the support he received, the importance of acknowledging that we are in God's hands, and how much he appreciates his neighbours.

9

CHARLOTTE'S STORY

INTERVIEW WITH CHARLOTTE WITH EMBEDDED COMMENTARY

Int: Can you talk through what happened after Paul died and especially about the people outside the family who helped.

Charlotte: This is really hard. I think in the first few days I think I was just in shock really. I just was convinced that I was just going to wake up the next day and he'd be there, you know, that it was just some weird dream that I would wake up from. And then you get focused on sorting out the funeral, so that sort of keeps you busy.

CHARLOTTE TELLS US that her initial response was one of shock and disbelief, but then practicalities took over.

When Paul died, my mother was there because she'd come up for the weekend and we were having the bathroom re-fitted and they'd done most of the work and we needed to paint and then they were coming to fit the fittings the following Monday. So, she'd been there, she was going to help me do that. And that was difficult in a way. I think it was like quite hard to, without sort of twenty-four hours, I just felt I didn't really want her there. So, I think she would have stayed for weeks if I'd wanted that. But it was quite hard to just say, actually we just need to be on our own, just the three of us.

Charlotte talks about domestic practicalities and links these with her need to be on her own, with her children (daughters – field notes).

There were people who really helped practically, who brought food and cooked for us and things in the first week or so and that was also helpful, because I had a sense of, although my girls aren't that young, you still end up feeling like you have to look after them, and part of me didn't want to have to look after anybody. Part of me just wanted to go and hide under a duvet really. So, it was really hard to do things like cook a meal. It if had just been me, I wouldn't have, I mean it just felt like such a mundane and inane task, but I felt I had to. So, people who were just dropping stuff off, that was helpful.

Charlotte reiterates her need to be alone, "by hiding under a duvet", but acknowledges that having two children necessitates looking after them. Charlotte is mixing emotion with practicalities and valuing those who support without being intrusive.

Int: Who were they?

Charlotte: Hilda, Sally and Margaret. They were the main people. Imelda. Things about the first few weeks or generally?

The interviewer prompts Charlotte to identify those who were supportive without being intrusive and Charlotte names four women. Charlotte checks with the interviewer and seeks clarification with regard to the timescale.

Int: First few weeks and afterwards.

Charlotte: O.K. So then my sister-in-law came up to help with the funeral preparations and that was good. It helped me interface to Paul's side of the family without having to have lots of conversations with lots of people. So in a practical sense, that was really, really practically very helpful. And I worked with the girls on organising the funeral. A woman minister and Ron were really helpful with the funeral arrangements and things. That was really nice and it was really special. It was important to Paul. He really wanted the woman minister to do it and that was really lovely. So I think those were the main things in terms of getting through the first fortnight really.

Charlotte expresses her gratitude to her sister-in-law who helped with the funeral preparations. Charlotte again, mixes her feelings of gratitude and values her sister-in-law's inter-personal sensitivity. We also see Charlotte appreciating the support of those who assist her in fulfilling her husband's wishes. In this section, we see Charlotte acknowledging the support of a family member, a woman minister and a male minister (Ron is a male minister – field notes)

And once the funeral was over, it was, it was a long journey really. I mean for many, many, many months I didn't really sleep very well and so over time I got more and more physically affected by that and it got more and more difficult to keep functioning. Through that time a number of people helped really. I think emotionally, the woman minister, Susannah and my friend Helen were really the only people I really talked to about how I was feeling.

She tells us that after the funeral it was a long journey. Charlotte tells us about how Paul's death affected her physically and emotionally. She cites three women whom she was comfortable enough to talk with about her emotions. So, Charlotte has spoken so far of three episodes: the shock of Paul's death; the funeral arrangements and the long journey post-funeral. Charlotte mixes emotion and practicality.

I found it, and even then I found it quite difficult to. My personality means that I find it really, past experience, it's just me. I find it really difficult to ask for help and so I tend to, if people ask me how I am, say "Yeah. I'm O.K. not too bad, up and down". You know those stock phrases, when inside you're thinking, actually I just feel like I want to go to sleep and never wake up again. But you just feel like you…So I think there were other people there who would have been there for me but I just didn't really find it easy to, even close friends like Sally and Margaret, didn't find it really easy to open up.

Charlotte talks about what she calls her struggle to open up to ask for help. She illustrates this difficulty by making reference to her responses to stock phrases and to her difficulty in sharing her feelings with some close women friends.

Int: What do you suppose it was that you felt you could talk to certain people and not others?

In exploring further why Charlotte felt that she could talk to some people and not to others the interviewer is following Charlotte's narrative.

Charlotte: I think for me it was actually they were less likely to try and think they could fix it. So like the woman minister, because she'd been through a similar experience and Susannah and Helen, my other two friends. Helen's been through a lot of other stuff and has battled with depression for quite a few years, many years. Yeah and Susannah because I think she's that sort of personality that I just had the sort of relationship with them where I knew that if I told them something, they weren't going to feel that they had to be responsible for making it better. I think that's what I found hard, why I find it hard to tell people because somehow it felt like if you told someone you weren't feeling good, that they would then feel that somehow they had to try and make you feel better or they had to find a solution and actually there is no solution and so I would feel like

I'm putting a burden on them, that they then feel like they have to do something and actually I'm not really asking them to do anything. I'm just asking them to listen. But some people don't get that and it's that idea that anyone's going to turn round and assume that they can fix what you're feeling. It just makes you feel like actually I just don't want to tell them anything really because actually you're not going to be able to fix it. So, I think that was what made the difference.

Charlotte, here, makes the point that she was talking to people who recognised that like Julian Barnes (2013), grief is not a thing that can be 'fixed'. She talked to people who she was confident would allow her to own her grief without trying to mend it in any way.

Int: Are you still being supported? What happened after?

Charlotte: It got….I did get iller and iller, so come February time, so that was four months later, I was diagnosed with depression and I started taking some medication, which helped a bit and then leading into that summer, I was still. So, I went back to work and then decided I wasn't going to go back to work, so I handed in my notice, but I worked my notice. So, I worked for my three months' notice, because I wanted to end it rather than just disappear. But having that end in sight and knowing that I wasn't going to have to be there all the time made it bearable. So, I got through, but that summer, you know, things continued to be quite difficult.

Charlotte is candid about the emotional turmoil she went through after Paul's death. Her grief was "medicalised" but she manages to find her own practical solution by deciding to stop work.

Eventually I think the things that helped in a way professionally, were I joined a bereavement group at the hospice, which was just six sessions over twelve weeks and I was with a lovely group of people and we still meet up now from time to time. Over the year we don't meet as often because we don't need to meet as often any more. And we had an amazing woman, Babs. She was our group leader. She was really, really helpful and I think that, you know, the starting point of that was just helping me, just suddenly understanding that this was normal and I wasn't going mad.

For Charlotte, joining a bereavement group helped enormously. She began to understand that how she was grieving was 'normal' and that she was not 'going mad'. It is interesting to note that she acknowledges that although initially the group met up every fortnight, they do not 'need' to meet up as frequently any more. Charlotte describes the leader of that group as being 're-ally, really helpful' and that she was an 'amazing woman'. (The field notes tell us that Babs is an Anglican minister)

I think that's what she..because I'd got to the point where I didn't really want to talk to anybody. I couldn't really have conversations. I was in meetings at work and I started having panic attacks and needing to get out of the room and I just found talking to people, like even a simple conversation, I'd get really, really anxious about it and I was having these real anxiety attacks, which is just so not my personality. I mean I can remember lying on the sofa and literally thinking I was going to die and so I thought I was going mad. So, it was really good to just be told, no, it's fine, that's what it's like. So that group was particularly helpful and we were able to carry on supporting each other afterwards as well, and again, I think the thing that everybody found with that group was it was just that sense of being able to talk about how you were feeling with people who sort of understood, so you realised that you weren't alone, but also that again, nobody was trying to fix it or tell you that it was going to get better or, you know. Not that you just want to wallow in it, but it's just it's a reality. It is what it is. So, and it's painful and it's hard to not. I don't know. It's not helpful to be trying to find solutions, particularly until…So that was particularly helpful and then that took me through into the summer.

Charlotte is very honest about her feelings and her state of mind during this next episode. She begins with the ordinary and moves on to what must have been very disturbing moments in her life. She talks about how comforting it was to be told that this "was what it's like" when grieving and that through being with the bereavement group, to learn that she could share these feelings with them without anybody trying to 'fix' it for her.

> *Then we went into the summer holidays and I think it was something to do with being holiday time basically and so I think how I coped a lot of the time was just to keep really busy. So, I did a lot of stuff and just kept filling my time and by the summer I'd given up work. It was the summer holidays so no-one was around and all the things that I normally filled my time with weren't happening and we weren't going on holiday. Cos Paul and I always looked forward to our holidays, that's one of the things that, cos I worked quite hard, actually holiday time was quite important to us. It was quite precious and we enjoyed spending our holidays together.*

Charlotte knew that the first summer without Paul would be difficult, so she filled it by keeping really busy, which she cites as a coping stratagem. Holiday times were very 'precious' to Charlotte characterised as they were by the enjoyment she, her husband, and daughters took in them.

> *So anyway, then I started some counselling at the local centre and I had a year's worth of counselling there because I'd been sort of supported loosely by them from when Paul was ill because we'd approached them for help with Mo really. Except Mo has refused ever to go and engage with them, so she never did but they offered me some counselling instead, so that was very nice of them. So, I met with Annie for a year and she was really helpful. So that was sort of professional help.*

The next episode in Charlotte's narrative involves what she calls 'sort of professional help'. Charlotte and her husband had initially approached the centre seeking help for Mo and she observes that they generously offered her counselling.

Int: What about people locally or friends?

The interviewer invites Charlotte to reflect on those who helped her and has worded the question to rephrase that when the interview opened.

Charlotte: So, Sally, Rick and Margaret were great and they took me away at Easter with them, which was really nice because it gave me some time out. One of the things I struggled with is and still do now, is feeling really lonely. So Sally and Rick and Margaret were great. I did spend quite a bit of time with them and they would take me out on day trips and things [and]

Charlotte talks about particular friends who took her away at Easter and also took her out on day trips. For the first time, Charlotte introduces the concept of being lonely.

[and] Paul died just before our wedding anniversary, so he died in October. We had the funeral a week later and a fortnight after that was our wedding anniversary and we obviously knew Paul was dying but we'd sort of expected that he would make our wedding anniversary, but not Christmas. That's sort of where we were at. And he obviously wasn't well enough to go away for our wedding anniversary, but what we'd arranged was that we booked a trip to France for the girls, so Sal and Mo went away and Paul and I were going to spend the weekend together on our own. But obviously Paul died before then but the trip was already booked, so Mo and Sal went that weekend and I spent some of that weekend at home on my own, which actually – and lots of people kept saying, "Come and do this. Come and do that." But actually, I wanted to be on my own. It was my first real opportunity just to sort of let go [and]

Charlotte goes back to the weeks immediately after Paul died and talks about her daughters going away, which meant she was left on her own, which was something she and Paul had arranged as they both knew it would be the last time they would share a wedding anniversary together.   She acknowledges that people knew she would be on her own and that they were concerned about that. However, Charlotte says that she needed that time just to be able to 'let go'.

> *[and] not be worrying about Sal and Mo and funnily enough it was Sal I worried about most. She had a real need for me to be O.K. It's like she felt this responsibility. So I felt in a sense, almost under a bit of pressure to be O.K. because I knew that if I didn't she would worry. She got very distressed if I was distressed.*

Charlotte goes on to talk about her worries about her daughters, and one in particular. Part of Charlotte's difficulty was that she had to appear to be 'all right' so as not to worry Sal, as she knew Sal was so empathetic. She ends up holding herself in for her daughter's benefit.

> *So, it was good to just have some peace to just sit and look at photos and cry, basically, and that's what I did. You know, you talked about not forgetting the memories. I just sat and went through years of photographs, just remembering, you know.*

For the first time Charlotte is able to spend just being on her own with her grief.

> *But I also went and stayed the first night with Margaret and then we went out the next day and did a load of Christmas shopping and then I came home and had that evening on my own. So, they were very good and I think again, I probably could have spent all my time with them, if you know what I mean. But that actually wasn't what I wanted to do. But it was hard as well because I felt like I also didn't want to feel like*

I was a burden on anybody, so I think there were definite times when I could have done with just spending some time with people but didn't really feel I wanted to ask anybody.

Charlotte admits she is finding herself pulled in two ways. She does not want to be a burden for anybody, she wants little spaces on her own and would value times spent with people who do not want to 'fix' anything.

Int: Have you actually come to terms with being on your own now?

Charlotte: I don't know that I have yet. It's funny, cos it feels like it goes in phases. So, the first phase was just learning how to deal with practical stuff and some of it wasn't about the fact that I couldn't do it; it was just the fact that I didn't do it and so it was things like getting my head round putting the bins out and then not getting angry about the fact that I had to put the bins out. Because Paul always put the bins out and suddenly I had to be bothered with like stuff like putting bins out. It was like, how come I got left putting the bins out? And you know, not having a meltdown every time a light bulb went in the kitchen because it's like this most stupid contraption of whoever designed the spotlight like that. I can't even reach it on a stepladder and it's just like, you know, you go through that phase of just having to do a load of stuff and do everything on your own and make all the decisions on your own. About O.K. it needs fixing but like are you going to fix it like this or like this? Well I don't know, just fix it, I don't care.

Charlotte begins by acknowledging the episodic nature of learning to be alone. It begins with her anger at having to put the bins out and continues with the light bulbs, because these were the things that Paul always saw to and she is now having to sort these out on her own as well as make decisions about maintenance in the home. She acknowledges her anger about the task and that leads to a certain amount of frustration with her circumstances.

And then the stuff about what I was going to do and things like that but I think now I'm at a stage where like we're going on holiday next week and it's the first time we'll have had a family holiday since Paul died. 'Cos I tried to book a holiday the following year and I just couldn't do it. I mean literally I was like at the point of booking the holiday and I just thought, I can't do this. So that's a milestone that we're going to actually just go on a family holiday this year without Paul. Next week. That's a big milestone to get to that but I feel like I have managed, and I am excited about going. I'm not dreading going and that's a big milestone. But I think the last bit in a way is that sense of just Mo's out more in the evenings now, increasingly and Sal, now that she's got a bit more settled and she's more confident about what she's doing.

Here, Charlotte introduces a new episode: one that involves going on holiday as a family, something she could not manage the previous year. She talks about this event as a 'milestone' in her life. She is excited about it and pleased that both her daughters are more settled.

Int: Has she moved into her new flat? (the interviewer had been told previously about the daughter's new flat – field notes)

Charlotte: No, not yet. But with that, basically I do spend more evenings on my own now and I know that, you know, twelve months from now, I'm going to be living in a different area, in a house on my own. Mo will be going off to college and actually I'm going to be moving to a place where people don't know me and I don't know people and actually, yeah, I feel that I don't know I'm going to be – it's going to be weird being, well it's going to be hard. But just that sense of, you know, when you go and do stuff, so as I've got better, I'm doing more things. But it's that sense of, so I can go out and I can enjoy myself now, which I found difficult in the beginning but when I come home I haven't got anyone to tell about it. I haven't got anyone to go, "Oh do you know what happened, oh it was really funny." Just those little conversations that you have. Paul was never a great one for going out anyway, but he was always there when I got back.

The interviewer uses information from an earlier meeting to ask a follow up question that hints at potential future loneliness. Charlotte acknowledges that both her daughters are leaving home and that takes her on to the fact that she, too, will be moving house. She is able to talk about going out and doing things and missing Paul when she comes home and has no-one to share her experiences with.

Int: Do you find it's sometimes the little nuances as well? You would know what each other is thinking?

Charlotte: Yeah. It's that intimacy, it's having someone that you're totally relaxed with and those moments, as you say, of just like knowing each other. And it is having someone to hang out with, that you're just totally relaxed with. And it is part of, we all have our baggage and part of my baggage from my childhood and things is I find it really hard to rely on people, so there's very few people that I'm really close to and Paul was the only person in the world ever that I've ever allowed to look after me, ever, and without that, you just have sense of feeling like really alone in the world. There isn't anybody there who is just the person that's there for you. So, yeah, I still find that really difficult.

The interviewer invites Charlotte to elaborate on the relationship she had with her husband. Charlotte responds by talking about her early childhood experiences and how, as a consequence, of this 'baggage' Paul was the only person she really opened up to, and she misses that and finds it really difficult. Charlotte is, here, talking about being 'alone' rather than being 'lonely'.

Int: Have you found that people you associate with are the same people you've always associated with or have you found you've gone towards people in a similar situation or are single. Have you kept contact with them more or less?

Here the interviewer invites Charlotte to reflect on her current friendships, which extends discussion from being alone to being with friends.

Charlotte: I think it is interesting that the one person I've made friends with at college is single. So, she's forty and single and never been married. So, from my existing friends, I think over time, I mean I see less of Sal and Rick now, in some ways. Just a bit less. It's difficult because I'm in a bit of a transition anyway but it's interesting, having gone to college, you know, the people I've ended up making friends with are more single. Cos it's really hard to be sort of, it's partly an age thing as well, cos the couples do tend to be a bit younger. The other thing that I've found, the odd change funnily enough, that really struck me is, I think partly because of my personality and partly because I've always worked in a fairly male-dominated environment, basically I've always had male friends. And I've found it harder to maintain a relationship with my male friends as it's almost like it's…

Int: Is it because you're single?

Charlotte: Yeah, if you know what I mean.

Int: It's taken away the safety catch?

Charlotte: I don't know really. It's sort of, I suppose it's a perception thing, isn't it? Whereas I suppose before Paul died, I would not think twice about going for a coffee or for a drink with the guys I know, on my own, just it wouldn't. Now it feels like I'm not really sure whether I should do that, you know. So that's weird.

Int: You don't want people to get the wrong impression?

Charlotte: Yes, I think that's what it is.

Int: Safeguarding yourself?

Charlotte: Yes.

Charlotte explains about now having to be more cautious in her dealings with men. Whereas before, when Paul was alive, she felt comfortable at going for a coffee or a drink with her male colleagues, now she feels uncomfortable and feels they may get the wrong impression of her. She now has one new female friend and has been struck by her move away from a male-dominated environment. **(couples' society)** The interviewer clarifies Charlotte's position with three short questions which at this point, indicates that the interviewer has understood Charlotte's responses.

Int: Talk about the support the church gave you.

Charlotte: Some of it was really good. A number of things. I mean I had some very practical support from some of the people in the church, so in the church family, you know.

Int: What sort of things?

Charlotte: Well like Dave and Alice, I mean Dave like just turned up, would just turn up and say, "Oh I've come to cut the grass" and things like that and that was really helpful. And there were some really good things, so when we got to the first anniversary because obviously I was working on the staff team by then and we were trying to organise a staff away day, an away few days, and they'd chosen the few days of Paul's, like the day that Paul's anniversary fell, so I e-mailed back and said, "No I can't do that week because that's the day of Paul's anniversary" and Ron went "Oh yeah", so he cancelled the away day and said, "Oh would you like to do a memorial service?", which we did and Paul's sister came up and

some friends and stuff and we had cake and it was just really lovely and
all the staff team came and I think we felt really supported in that and it
was really lovely.

The quiet kindness of church members was very much appreciated by
Charlotte. She then goes on to talk about Paul's first anniversary. She really
appreciates the memorial service held for Paul and the fact that the away day
was cancelled. She also appreciates that there was cake and that friends and
family members, as well as the staff team, came to the service and the refresh-
ments afterwards.

I think there were other times when I felt like, and again this is linked to,
I find it really difficult to ask for help, but there were times when I was
feeling really rough and so I might cancel. Say it was a Tuesday morning
and we were doing staff prayers or whatever and I might send a text and
say, "look I just can't come today, you know, really feeling, you know" Or
say, "I've had a bit of a crash so I can't come or whatever to a meeting"
or I might cancel something. And like nobody would ring me or send a
text later in the day to say, "how are you doing?" and that really upset me.
I felt like actually, at the time I felt like you don't care about me. And
again, I think it is partly because I come across quite self-sufficient, but
I think there were times when I indicated that I wasn't feeling and I felt
people could have followed up a bit more.

Charlotte goes on with an attempt to carry the blame for lack of support as a
consequence of her own difficulties in asking for help. This leads to the other
side of the coin where she admits her own difficulties and shares them but
gets no support. She suggests this might be her fault for presenting herself as
self-sufficient. Nonetheless she feels those in the church might have followed
up her messages.

Int: Do you feel you're supported at college or is it something you've not
dwelt on at college?

Charlotte: My tutor is really good. His name's Harold. He's my tutor and he is lovely and he's been really supportive and there's been times when I haven't been able to like do stuff that I'm supposed to do. I can text him and I know that he just understands and he always reassures me that it's absolutely fine, just do what you need to do and he'll always follow up and check how I am and he's really good. Our pastoral tutor, the person who's responsible for the chaplain, the person who's responsible for pasturing is rubbish. She's also the one who teaches pastoral theology and she's just like the most un-pastoral person I've ever met in my life…she's just horrendous. So literally my first week at college was, so the first day of lectures was a friend's funeral. So, and the induction week was the week before. Now there was a whole load of stuff in induction about what you have to do if you're going to miss a lesson and you've got to contact your tutor and stuff. Well my tutor was still abroad, because he was coming back a week late, he was doing some lecture engagement out there. So, I went to the tutor, as the pastoral person, thinking well I can't speak to my tutor, so I'll come to you, and said, "look I've got to miss the first lecture next week because I've got to go to a funeral. I will get back in time for the second lecture" and considering she knows me, she knows my situation in full, there was no sense of, oh that's a funeral, that might be a bit difficult for Charlotte. Instead it was like, well you do realise that you have to attend 80% of lectures in order to pass and so if you don't go to that one, then you, and I thought, actually she was just horrendous, absolutely horrendous. No sensitivity whatsoever and just made me feel like a complete slacker. And I'm thinking, oh she was, and she's been like that all the way through really and not just with me. She really is poor. (Pause)

Apart from that, generally the environment I think is not. I feel that I've had some good support from my colleagues. I've got two girls that I'm in a prayer triplet with and we really support each other and that's been really helpful during the year as well. I think the college is a bit inflexible sometimes, around the college day, as it were. But I think a lot of people feel that for all sorts of reasons. It doesn't really cope with changing the fact that they're not all twenty-something year old single people living on site. There's a sort of sense that you've got nothing else to do but be at college. You will be there at 8.30 every morning and you will be there at all these things and you know, every so often they'll have a, but there's no sort of sense of actually, you can't always be there at 8.30 every morning, you know.

Charlotte's college narrative has four elements to it. Firstly, the understanding and sensitivity of her own tutor is warmly appreciated. But then, Charlotte goes on to recount an episode which she found very challenging, being related to bereavement, where her pastoral tutor's response to her needs was described as 'absolutely horrendous'. She feels the general environment of the college is based on a rather outmoded assumption that all students are youngsters who live on the campus and actually there is little flexibility for older, mature students with family responsibilities. The fourth element is the good support she receives from her colleagues and here she gives an example of two girls she is in a prayer triplet with.

Int: There is life outside?

Charlotte: There is life outside. Some days Mo's having a mad half hour, takes a while to get her going in the morning, you know and. Except my tutor, my own tutor's very good. He will understand, but the rest of the college environment, it's not sort of quite so forgiving.

The interviewer checks her interpretation of Charlotte's heart-felt commentary. Charlotte confirms that she has family commitments that occasionally take precedence over punctuality. Again, she emphasises the understanding of her own tutor in contrast to that found in the general college environment.

Int: Did you find it easier to talk to women or men about Paul's death?

Charlotte: I think I'd say I don't think I thought about it that way but what was interesting is, so I don't think I have an issue either way. But it was interesting that most of the people I spoke to were women. But I think that's just because there were a lot more women, both associated with that environment, so all the, you know, my counsellor was a woman, the person who ran my group was a woman, all that sort of stuff. I think women tend to be more drawn to those pastoral, they're more likely to ask you how you're feeling. So, it's not that I felt I couldn't speak to a man, but it's just that I don't think I got into many conversations with them, if you see what I mean.

The interviewer recognises that Charlotte has confirmed the interviewer's interpretation of Charlotte's college context and goes on to explore Charlotte's experiences of gendered responses to grief. Charlotte says that although it was not an issue for her 'either way', in her experience virtually everybody with whom she spoke, who was in a caring or supportive role, happened to be a woman. In her experience, then, it was women who occupied every pastoral role.

Int: Did you ever have any crass conversations with people?

Charlotte: Yes a couple. I had one conversation and this has been nearly a year ago so, with actually one of my friends and one of the people who's been quite supportive all the way through and we'd gone out for a drink and she decided to ask me whether I wanted to do on-line dating and did I want some help from her doing on-line dating.(Laughs) *Apparently she'd supported a couple of friends before. Just thought that was too.*(Laughs)

At the end of Charlotte's confirmation, the interviewer initiates a prompt change of subject with a personal question.

Charlotte singles out one crass conversation for comment which actually came from an otherwise supportive friend. She laughs about the inappropriateness of the offer of help with on-line dating.

Int: Can people not come to terms with the fact you are now single, and that you shouldn't be and should have a partner?

Charlotte: Yeah, I think so. Yes, I think there is a sense that, (Pause) almost like an assumption. So I think there are those that you think that you should, like this person and then I think there are those that just assume, that at some point, like my sister, who just assume, when you're ready, you know. And I'm not saying that that's not the case but it's interesting that there's an assumption that at some point you will look for a partner again.

The interviewer suggests that people in general may have difficulties recognising that Charlotte is not bothered about her status as a single person. Rather she dismisses the attempts of others to reinstate her to 'coupledom'.

Int: How do you feel about that?

Charlotte: I don't know. I can't imagine doing that at the moment. But you know, life's a long time. I do see, rather than feel, I do see that I've become increasingly single, if that makes sense, but that's more in other people's perceptions of me than how I feel. But I know that that is a reality. You see, when I move to a new parish next year, there'll be nobody there who knew Paul, there'll be nobody there who knew me as a couple. And that feels weird. But it's a reality that I have to learn with. Because you have those conversations when people ask you what your partner does, somebody did that last week when we were away and you know, those can sometimes be awkward conversations. Not for me, but for them. I usually turn round and go, "I'm a widow", and they go "Oh, I'm so sorry" But it tends to make people feel uncomfortable. I don't mean to do that but at the same time I think, well I'm not just going to go, "Yeah". And that increasingly happens again, as you meet people who don't know you.

The interviewer pursues Charlotte's perceptions to the responses of others because it provides insight into how personal grief can be morphed into social convention. Charlotte remains open-minded whilst recognising that she sees herself as single, others may not. She then goes on to reflect on the potential strangeness of moving to a new context where others will not have known her socially as part of a 'couple'. She is also reflecting on the potential implications of grief inherent in describing herself as a widow.

Int: Did you ever feel you had to reinvent yourself?

Charlotte: No.(Pause) *I don't feel I need to reinvent myself, but I do feel,*(Pause) *I found it difficult at the beginning and still do to some extent, being with people who don't know Paul, didn't know us as a couple because it's like and it sounds weird, because it's not like I'm this, you know, flower of a woman that only had her identity in her husband sort of thing, as you well know. But it's a huge part of me. It's like you don't live with someone for twenty seven years without, in a sense, and you know, we'd been together since I was eighteen, so all my adult life, I'd shared with him and so we'd, in a sense been shaped by each other and so when I meet new people, it's like I feel they don't know me. Because there's this part of me that they don't know and it's weird introducing yourself. It's like you're getting to know somebody but it feels like they're only getting to know a half of you, if you know what I mean. It feels like there's this bit that they're not getting to know and they should. But it's hard to do that without keep over-running the story and also it's like, I don't want to be defined as a victim. I don't want to be defined as a widow, but at the same time, I find it quite hard not to, hard or weird?*

The interviewer pursues Charlotte's concern with the responses of others to her grief by asking Charlotte whether she feels the need to 'reinvent' herself. This prompts Charlotte to think carefully about the question. There are two pauses and four beginnings through which Charlotte generates some powerful reflections on the creation of self-identity in relation to a life-partner and the sudden loss of that life-partner. Charlotte recognises that on the one hand her identity was never entirely bound with that of her husband's; while on the other, acknowledging that people who did not know him do not fully 'know' her because she and her husband had 'shaped' each other. So, now, unable to know him, they cannot fully 'know' her. This, in turn, makes self-introduction problematic. Charlotte is confident in acknowledging that she is a widow and because of this she rejects any positioning of her as a 'victim'.

It's that sense of I don't sit there and tell everybody I meet, knew about everything that happened to me because I don't want to be defined, I'm, not a victim. But by not doing that, I feel like I'm not really getting to know them or they're not really getting to know me. Do you know what I mean, it's sort of, it's like there's this whole part of me that they're not sharing and that's quite weird, sort of yeah, in a way of developing new relationships, you know. And I suppose I'm in a strange situation in a sense, because I gave up work and then I started training. Actually, I am meeting a whole load of new people that I might not otherwise have done and I'm not spending most of my time in my old circles. I'm actually spending a lot of time in new circles and that's a sort of circumstance but actually it makes for a different dynamic, I think.

Charlotte goes on to reflect on issues of identity and being known to others which she sees as problematic when developing new relationships. She is telling us that this is particularly pertinent to her because her circumstances have led her to meet lots of new people. She feels that identifying herself in this way produces a 'different dynamic'.

Int: Is there anything else you want to add? (The interviewer identifies the Kubler-Ross stages and the Stroebes Dual Process Model – field notes) *How did you feel – did you go through to acceptance or oscillating?*

Charlotte: I think I went in and out of the different stages. I have looked at stages of grieving and I think they're not stages, as I didn't go through

one and then the other and then the other. I just bounced about in be-
tween them and some days, yes, some days were better and some days were
awful and I suppose now I have more good days than I have bad days, in
the sense of that balance is getting better.

The interviewer is confident that Charlotte will be able to accommodate some
theoretical perspectives on grief and Charlotte responds with a thoughtful
critical self-reflection. She reframes 'oscillation' as 'bouncing' and rejects a
sequential account of grief.

But I still can be really angry, I can still feel all of those emotions again at
any time. I mean I remember feeling really angry with Paul at one point,
this is quite an early one. I think it was when I was ill and my brain was
a bit all over the place but you know this thing about hope, you know, as
Christians we've got hope and we know that when we come into heaven
that there'll be, there's that phrase, you know, there's no more tears, no
more grief, no more pain, no more suffering and I remember thinking,
that's all right for you. I remember thinking, this is really not fair be-
cause Paul's in heaven and there's no grief in heaven, therefore he can't
be grieving that we're not with him. But we're grieving, and I remember
getting really angry about that and I laugh about it now, but at the time,
it was just like, it's not fair, you know. How did you get off this?

Charlotte identifies anger and acknowledges a range of emotions that she can
feel at any time. She tells us that she can still feel the emotional totality that
is grief but she returns to her anger. Her faith tells her that her husband is in
heaven and that means he is safe from grief and Charlotte can be angry that
her and her daughters are not, and are still suffering.

Cos that was, I remember that, because I remember some, you were talk-
ing about crass comments, that's the other one. You know, that you've got
your faith, so therefore it's all O.K., which was basically what the person
was saying and I said, "Well it doesn't quite work like that really."

Charlotte brings to mind the second crass conversation she had where the person in question assumed that because Charlotte had a faith everything was therefore all right. Charlotte quickly responded that faith was not that simple.

Yeah, so I think I can still oscillate through those now. It's just a bit less and a bit in a different dimension. I mean, back in July, just one day, I got up and I woke up and just realised and I don't know what it was that brought it to mind cos it's not, you know, you have like this thing about anniversaries so you get through your first Christmas and then the first birthday and it's Paul's birthday and it's Father's Day and what are we going to do and how are we going to mark these things, and I woke up, it was the beginning of July and this is three years now, and I just suddenly realised, it was three years today that we went to see the consultant and that he said: "There's nothing more that we can do and it'll be a matter of months." And I was just like, it floored me, you know, I was ill for two days and just it was like being back in it all again, you know, back to day one, absolute grief and everything. And yet that's not an anniversary we'd ever marked. I mean I've never recognised that date in the two years previous. And it just came completely out of the blue.

Charlotte tells us that she is still subject to oscillating through different kinds of grief. She tells us that these feelings are just a bit less and in a 'different dimension' which she goes on to illustrate by citing the anniversary of the day that she remembers receiving the news from the consultant that Paul was not going to live. This came to her totally unexpectedly and was not like remembering other anniversaries such as Father's Day or birthdays, in that it took her back to the overwhelming feelings of absolute grief that she had had about a time not previously commemorated by her.

Int: You then had a time limit, which is dreadful.

Charlotte: Yeah and it was, yeah and I think at the time it was an important date because up until that point we always assumed Paul would

get better, you know. We'd never considered that he wouldn't get better.
It was all about getting through something. But I don't think it had
ever, emotionally we'd never registered that he wouldn't get better. So
that was, that, you know and that was just this year, you know and just
the other day I was thinking that it'll be thirty years this year that we
met. Well not that we met, that we started going out. Thirty years this
October. All those years, which makes me feel really old as well, but..

The interviewer acknowledges that this was the moment when Paul's life expectancy was made explicit. For Charlotte, this is a significant date because there was to be no recovery and Paul was going to die in the foreseeable future. Three years later she recognises the significance of this date for the first time. This takes her on to recalling when they first went out together.

Yeah, so basically yes, I don't think you go through these phases in a linear
way. I think you jump around and it still surprises me sometimes how
deep the pain can be, you know. As I say it is not as regular and it does
often take me by surprise. I can be doing and then suddenly, I mean
actually I had, just this Sunday, a really, I was preaching at a church
and I included some of my testimony about how God walked with me
after Paul died, when I was feeling really ill, as part of the sermon and
when I did it I was absolutely fine and I don't know how much it was
just re-visiting that in order to write and deliver the sermon or whether
it was because somebody came up to me afterwards and, you know, just
to say like thank you, I really needed to hear that today and talked a bit
about someone, a young woman with a history, and so I don't know if it
was that as well, but I got home, Sal was away. I thought I can't get my
head round food so I just took Mo down to a café and we had some lunch
and then I sort of like just dragged myself through and tried to get her to
go upstairs and do some work, partly because she had to do some work,
but also because I just needed her out of the way and I just crashed and
I think for about twelve hours I just laid on the sofa and watched T V.
episode after episode after episode of NCIS. Then Mo came down about

a quarter to ten, she said, "Just on the phone to Roxanne, she said she'd ring me back at ten and I've realised it's a quarter to ten and we haven't had any dinner." So, I said, "Oh there's some bolognaise in the fridge if you want to put it in the microwave" and she said, "Oh I won't bother to do that." She said, "Can I have some cereal?" I said, "Yes, fine." I said, "Actually you can get me a bowl of cereal." So, we both had that. She said, "We're like students." We had a bowl of cereal for our tea and then she went back to bed and then I ended up falling asleep on the sofa. I woke up eventually, I fell asleep and woke up and actually I was fine the next day, but I just, you know, couldn't do anything.

In her concluding remarks, Charlotte rejects a linear progression through phases of grief. Charlotte's grief remains with her. She has described this variously as oscillating, bouncing, jumping around, sudden, and taking her by surprise. Grief is still capable of summoning up deep pain for her. Charlotte reflects that in the process of considering how God has been beside her in her life; in writing, in preaching about it and then hearing the related testimony of another, simply floors her. She concludes this telling episode by recalling a joke her daughter made about them living off cereal like students.

WHAT DOES CHARLOTTE TELL US ABOUT GRIEF?

A SENSE OF CHRONOLOGY

Charlotte gives us a very personal chronology in which she identifies her phases of feeling. The first phase she identifies is that of shock and disbelief. Then she goes on to say practicalities soon took over. She links her talk about domestic practicalities with her need to be on her own. Charlotte begins a pattern of mixing emotion and practicalities and valuing those who support without being intrusive. Given her concerns with practicalities it does not surprise us that for Charlotte the funeral's preparations come next and are valued both because she meets Paul's side of the family and because, as she emphasises, the service was very special to her.

Here, she values the support of two women and one man. Following the service Charlotte tells us she went on a 'long journey'. She identifies three women who helped her through this emotional terrain. They were the only people she really talked to about her feelings. It is not clear that Charlotte considers the 'long journey' over. She tells us how her grief was medicalised and how she helped herself by stopping work and joining a bereavement group, what she calls 'professional help'. Here she especially valued an 'amazing woman' (an Anglican minister). In her re-telling, she revisits what must have been some very disturbing moments in her life. Charlotte speaks of extreme loneliness and about the friends (two women and a man) who helped through Easter and beyond. She filled her first summer, without Paul, by keeping really busy, but admits that it was a really hard time as holidays were so precious to her and Paul.

FACING UP TO GRIEF

It is clear that Charlotte struggles with her grief. Although, as she tells us, that she had been on a 'long journey', which was not accomplished alone, Charlotte's grief remains with her and it still takes her by surprise. She speaks of generous specialist help; at the same time, she values being with people who do not want to 'fix' anything. There were times when grief overwhelmed her and she thought she was 'going mad'. On other occasions, she resorted to climbing under her duvet or watching endless episodes of a crime series on television. She speaks of being unable to have conversations, of having panic attacks in meetings, and of getting very anxious about even simple conversations. These real anxiety attacks contributed to her feelings that she was 'going mad'. Being told that that was not the case, that it was fine to feel anxious, to worry about simple conversations and to continue to grieve "that's what it's like" reassured her that she was not the only one to experience such feelings. She speaks of not wallowing in grief but of its painful reality. Charlotte tells us that it is not helpful to try and find solutions for grief.

The bereavement group mentioned above was, in Charlotte's view, particularly helpful. Charlotte also talks about the time when she felt angry with her husband for leaving them behind, whilst he was peacefully in heaven, and not having to cope with the grief that she and her daughters were undergoing. She describes this as 'not fair'. On another occasion, Charlotte talks about 'remembering' when she spends time on her own, looking at photos, remembering happier times with Paul and her daughters.

The interviewer felt it appropriate to share two analyses of grief; one that was predicated on stages of grief and the other that was a dual process model, which deals with, among other things, the concept of "oscillation". Charlotte picked up on the oscillation and described herself as not going through particular stages, but of bouncing, jumping around and being taken by surprise between emotional states.

Reflections on support from the Anglican community

Charlotte's first response is that some support was "really good", particularly the very "practical support" which showed the quiet kindness of church members whom she describes as "in the church family". She appreciated the memorial service that was held for Paul and sharing cake with friends and family members as well as the staff team. Any lack of support is in Charlotte's view, her own fault, arising from her reluctance to share her feelings. Nonetheless, she feels that those in the church might have followed up her messages during times of a deep personal struggle with grief. As a consequence of this, she felt "you don't care about me". She goes on to express her appreciation for the support given by the female Anglican minister who led the bereavement counselling group.

Because Charlotte was attending a denominational college, this seems an appropriate place to reflect on the support Charlotte received. She found some tutors incredibly supportive, almost a model of good pastoral care; whilst others seemed to find it difficult to respond appropriately to a mature woman suffering a profound personal loss. Charlotte found her fellow students genuinely supportive, which she really appreciated.

ON BEING A WIDOW

Charlotte reflects on her experiences of missing her husband, of being a widow. Charlotte also reflects on how she describes herself and choosing when to say that she is a 'widow'.

The first of these is characteristic of Charlotte's narrative in the way that she mixes mundane practicalities with a deep sense of emotional loss. She will speak of the practicalities of putting the bins out and changing the light bulbs, once an activity that her husband undertook, now a marker of his absence and her loss. Related to this is the loss of her husband, who had that special affectionate understanding, when she came home from work in the evening and shared her day.

The second of these arises in everyday conversations, when people ask, "what your partner does", which normally elicits a response of "oh I'm so sorry" and that tends to make people feel uncomfortable.

These reflections lead Charlotte to speculate on life in a social context where nobody has known her as part of a couple. So, her marriage was a huge part of her. Having lived with her husband for twenty-seven years she felt, in a sense, they had been 'shaped' by each other. Charlotte recognises that her identity was never entirely bound with that of her husband but she also feels that those who did not know him, are now unable to fully know her. Charlotte is confident in acknowledging that she is a widow and because of this rejects any attempt to position her as a victim.

Charlotte also reflects on being lonely and that is something she still finds very hard. She says there are definite times 'when she could have done with spending time with people', yet she did not feel able to ask anybody in case she was a 'burden' to anybody. On the other hand, there were times when she really needed to be 'alone' so that she could have time to grieve, time to reflect and time to cry if she needed to. She distinguishes quite clearly between these two states as, for her, they are two separate entities. Being on your own, for

Charlotte, is learning to deal with the practicalities whereas being lonely is a 'feeling that comes and goes'. However, she does go on to say that without someone you were really close to (in this case Paul) being around for you, 'you just have the sense of being really alone'. Being alone in this case is much more to do with being a widow than with being lonely, which anyone can be.

REFLECTIONS ON GENDER

Charlotte is very capable of grasping the issue of gender as it affects her in becoming a widow.

First of all, she appreciates four, named women who really helped her practically. She then goes on to reference one woman minister who was especially important and one male minister who was supportive at the time of the funeral. In her subsequent long journey, she cites three women with whom she was comfortable enough to talk about her emotions. As we have noted, she found the woman minister, who organised the bereavement group, as especially helpful. She goes on to identify three helpful members of the church family, two women and one man, who were both emotionally and practically supportive. Later on, she mentions a couple who came round uninvited and quietly cut her grass and 'things like that', which for Charlotte were really helpful.

At college, it was a male tutor who was really helpful and a female who was 'horrendous'. She also found two women students with whom she prayed, to have been supportive and helpful during the year.

SOME PERSONAL DISCURSIVE FEATURES

Charlotte, throughout her discourse moves between the practicalities of coping with grief and the emotional impact these practicalities trigger. Sometimes this is to acknowledge the support of others; sometimes it is to reflect on the feelings of grief they trigger.

On five occasions during her narrative, Charlotte uses the word 'weird'. It is often linked to a social context and having been part of a couple. Having to reject the labels that others might pin on her is described by Charlotte as 'weird'.

Charlotte occasionally uses repetitions for emphasis. For example, she talks about not sleeping for 'many, many, many' months. The funeral arrangements were 'really, really' practically very helpful and it was 'really' nice and 'really' special. Later, she speaks of the help she receives from the bereavement group leader as 'really, really' helpful.

10

ELLIE'S STORY

INTERVIEW WITH ELLIE WITH EMBEDDED COMMENTARY

Int: Talk through what happened after your husband died – especially those people outside your family who helped you most during those difficult days.

Ellie: Right, well my husband died at night, and he was taken to the hospital and I was trying to get hold of my sister. My sister and I are really close, then eventually I did manage to get hold of her and she lives about eighty miles from here, so she came up from her home. And then we were told Nick had passed away. So I did have Abbie and my son was fourteen at the time and so he was leaning on each of us. But my sister, she helped me with all the funeral arrangements. In the back of the leaflet or the booklet from the undertakers it had people to contact, you know, like banks and things like that, which I found really helpful.

ELLIE BEGINS WITH 'Right, well' and that tells us that she is thinking back to the night that Nick died. This takes her away from the interviewer's question and directly to those members of her family who helped her, especially her sister and her son. Then she returns to the question and tells us that the undertaker was particularly helpful and the booklet he gave her especially helpful.

Ellie: I'd done everything for the next couple of months informing banks, building societies and everything and obviously the gas and electric and the house needed to get put into my name. But the backbone was my sister. She would come round whenever she could, bearing in mind it was from a fair distance. She would stay over when she could, I was working at the time, people at my workplace didn't know I had MS until Nick passed away. Of course, that hit me like a brick wall, with MS you go down. So, the friends at work – my best friend we used to do everything together. My husband used to, 'cos he worked nights, he used to come home and give me and my friend who lived just nearby a lift into work. And as time went by, obviously we had to make our own arrangements to get into work and I found that she was, not so close to me, it was almost as though, if I couldn't do something for her, she wouldn't support me. So, I know. That's a good best friend isn't it? Yeah, the next couple of months after Nick passed away I was writing to people, obviously to tell them that he'd passed away. Abbie, yes, was still hanging about, bless her. I did end up having counselling. I didn't want counselling, but the lady that came, 'cos she came for I think it was four sessions and at the end of it, I could smile again.

Ellie tells us that she dealt with all the practicalities of registering herself as responsible for her home and its utilities. Again, she talks about her sister and about how helpful she was.

She then goes on to talk about having Multiple Sclerosis (MS) and about how her MS amplified the grief following Nick's death. She provides an ironic commentary on an apparent 'best friend'. Her sister, on the other hand, was still there for her. Then she goes back to people outside the family and talks about the positive outcome of her unwanted counselling after which she could 'smile again'.

Int: Oh, how lovely!

Ellie: which I thought that was really good. And people have said that when I talk about my husband, I smile a lot, 'cos he was like my soul mate. But, yeah, family were there to support me. Friends, work friends and that – they all sort of dwindled away.

The interviewer validates Ellie's experience. This dialogic exchange leads Ellie to say more about her late husband and how her fond memories of her 'soul mate' make her smile. What is happening here is that the interviewer leads Ellie to re-validate and extend her previous statement. This extension goes on to reaffirm the continuing support of family whilst recognising fading away of previous friendships.

Int: O.K.

Ellie: And after a year of coming to terms with things, I think people think, 'Oh, they'll be all right now', that is when you actually need people the most. 'Cos you don't want to feel sort of left out on a limb sort of thing. Yeah.

Ellie first identifies the false assumptions others make (perhaps those who have not experienced grief of this kind) about her having managed a year without Nick and goes on to say that it is at this point that she felt she needed people more than ever, and she attributes this to not wanting to be left 'out on a limb'.

And then, my husband and I were going to move down to be with my family because that's where all my family are from. But Sam, that's my son, he got into college and he said if I moved, he would have to manage a change of trains from there to his college and that was going to be too much of an upheaval.

Nick's death led Ellie to postpone their plans to move, especially as a response to changes in Sam's education plans.

So, many moons passed, I'm still here. I'm not with my family. He's now working for a really good supportive company for him, so that is really good, but yeah, he passed his exams at school and everything. We support each other; we do talk about my husband; we've still got his ashes. Sam doesn't want to scatter them yet and I respect Sam because if he doesn't want to, because we are a team, a family, and I won't do anything with the ashes until he's ready.

Sam's wish that they retain Nick's ashes for the time being is part of Ellie's conception of working as a family team, which is really important for her.

Int: It's important isn't it, being seen working as a team, then you know everybody is comfortable with what you decided.

Ellie: Yep, and it's like Sam and I went through in to see the coffin and did everything together, and we went and saw Nick you know. Sam and I are close, but that made us even closer. So yes, my little boy who's all grown up now.

The interviewer checks on the importance of team work and the comfort it offers arrangements following Nick's death. She tells us that this has drawn her and her son closer together and concludes with another ironic joke.

Int: How about your daughter?

Ellie: I haven't got any other family; it's just Sam.

Int: Just Sam

Ellie: Just Sam

Int: Lovely

Ellie: But that girl you saw on the stairs was Sam's partner

Int: Oh right, lovely

Ellie: Obviously Naomi is his daughter

In this exchange, the interviewer somehow clarifies an error and an understanding of family relationships.

Int: That's nice.

Ellie: And they live here which I like because as I say, because Nick's not here, it's nice to have somebody to talk to. I used to clock watch on a Friday, twenty past seven. That is when Nick would finish his work, he would come home and then the weekends were for us and I had one work colleague – he said you're never going to clock watch again. I'm going to make sure we go out every Friday and he did. And he's moved in, but yeah, strange how things work out.

The interviewer values family arrangements and this leads Ellie to an expansion in which she is able to move from the present to the past and back to the present again.

Int: Yes, that's lovely. What about the friend locally; couldn't she offer you a lift into work? Were there any other friends outside the family who supported you and helped you at the time?

Ellie: There were a couple of work colleagues, there were two managers that actually would pop in every now and again, and I had two visitors from - it was two men that I used to work with, but apart from that, nobody else, nobody. Even my manager at the time didn't even say I'm sorry to hear that your husband had passed away or anything, he just kept shtum.

Ellie's experience of support post-bereavement is unusual in that it is men who used to pop in to see her whilst otherwise nobody would mention Nick's death.

Int: Some people find it very embarrassing don't they?

Ellie: Yeah, they, they don't know what to do, do they?

Int: No. Those people that you mentioned who supported you most, what was it that they said or did that made that difference, special difference at the time, sympathy, empathy, enabling you to talk about grief, I'm not feeding you, but thinking along those lines.

Ellie: I mean my sister was there, she was somebody to hold my hand, if I wanted to have a good old cry. Abbie was there. And she sometimes would join in as well. But, yeah, Abbie helped because I wanted to do all the paper and that, paperwork by myself. I wasn't going to pass it on to a solicitor or anything. So that kept me busy, kept my mind occupied. Abbie would advise me if I wanted any advice, so would my mum, because my mum had to do exactly the same thing when my dad passed away. But, no, it was mainly my sister. Not very many people from my work came.

The interviewer raises the embarrassment of others which Ellie endorses and attributes it to lack of understanding. The interviewer goes on to elaborate possible areas for discussion. Ellie goes straight to her sister who was able to sometimes join her in a good cry. Ellie then talks about the importance of post-bereavement paperwork in keeping her occupied and the importance of her sister and her mum in helping her cope with this.

Int: Do you still work?

Ellie: No, no. No, I did start work again last year in June, but then I gave it up because I thought so, this MS is horrible. Apart from that it was mainly my sister.

Int: Being bereaved can mean loneliness. Were you helped in any way to be able to come to terms with being on your own?

Ellie: I was offered counselling, but I said no. And it wasn't until I'd sort of gone back to work then it had been brought up in a meeting, I thought (coughs) excuse me, I'll go for the counselling and that was one of the best things I could have done.

Int: What made the difference?

Ellie: Talking to a complete stranger, them not bothered if you burst into tears, or didn't want to talk about anything. They'd be there and they'd listen. They wouldn't force their opinion on you or anything, they were more interested in what you had to say and at the end of it you're given like a little card that got filling in, you'd write something down. I said thank you and I said that this lady actually helped me to smile again because she's she was excellent. I can't say exactly how she helped me but she listened and she was there.

Int: It's the listening that is so important.

Ellie: It is, oh yes. I mean you don't have to have somebody crying and holding your hand, saying 'Oh I know what you're going through'

Int: They do though! Quite!

Ellie: And it's good just to be able to express yourself; talk; cry if you want to have a cry; not being looked at or judged. It was good counselling. I'd recommend it to anybody.

Int: Where did you get the counsellors from?

Ellie: The doctor suggested it in the beginning. I said, no, and it was through work because I used to work and that was their HR department that suggested it.

Int: Oh right

Ellie: So I did.

There is a brief piece of factual detail about Ellie's work situation and then the interviewer goes on to ask about loneliness and about coming to terms with being on her own. Ellie goes back to talking about her experience with counselling and reiterates that it was one of the 'best things' she could have done. The interviewer prompts Ellie to say more. Ellie continues by discussing the counselling in greater detail, mentioning in particular the advantage of being with a complete stranger who is able to listen, not judge, nor comment about Ellie's situation. It was the presence of another who was prepared to simply listen, allow her to cry and ultimately to smile again. The interviewer and Ellie contrast good counselling with those well-meaning people who claim empathy which the interviewer agrees with. That leads Ellie to expand on not being judged for having a good cry. She endorses good counselling, provided by her employer, by saying she would recommend it to anyone.

Int: What sort of funeral did your husband have?

Ellie: It was, he was cremated, because it all happened so quick. The death was unexpected, really unexpected and because I, funnily enough that day we had actually spoken about death and he said, 'I'm going to go before you' and I said, 'No, I said I'll go before you,' and we had a conversation which was light hearted but to the point, not knowing that that night my husband was going to drop down dead. So I didn't know any hymns or anything to do at the service. The service was not by anybody that we knew.

Int: Wasn't by anybody that you knew or was?

Ellie: It was anybody there, anybody that was there was either my work colleagues, Nick's work colleagues, friends, family.

Int: Who conducted the service?

Ellie: It was a very nice Reverend, but I can't remember his name. But a year later my mother-in-law died and he done her service as well.

Int: Oh, that's nice.

Ellie: So that was really good. The same undertakers as well, and, it's funny how you don't expect undertakers to recognise you, but the undertaker recognised me and gave me a hug.

Again, there is a clarification activity in which the person who led the service is identified. Ellie goes on to say that the same minister and the same funeral directors assisted at her mother-in-law's funeral and how an undertaker recognised and comforted her at the second funeral.

Int: How lovely

Ellie: So

Int: Oh, that's kind.

Ellie: Good, yes. But yeah, it was, it was a nice service and because my husband was in the services, he had at the end a services specific tune or song, whatever you like to call it.

Int: Yes. Did the person that conducted the service, did he go through the service with you and discuss what you wanted?

Ellie: Yes

Int: Good. Did you do that with your son as well?

Ellie: I, I don't think so. I think he was at school. So. But yeah, we got everything that we wanted to say.

Int: Good, yes.

Ellie: But one of the hardest things was because Nick's mum and dad were there. And obviously they were supporting me as well as I was supporting them. It was, it was hard. It was hard.

Int: Yes

Ellie: So you should never, your children should never die before you.

Int: Yes, there's always that isn't there?

Ellie: Yeah

The interviewer discusses the format of the service with Ellie and establishes that Nick's parents were present at the discussion, but that her son was not. She recognises how hard it must have been for Nick's parents as well as for herself and that they were able to mutually support each other.

Int: The Reverend – did you have any contact with him afterwards at all or not?

Ellie: No, but he did give me his card and said, 'if you need to talk to me, you can phone me, there's my number.'

Int: O.K. was he approachable?

Ellie: Yes

The interviewer asks Ellie about any post-bereavement support she had from the minister who conducted Nick's funeral service. Ellie confirms the minister was very approachable, and that he offered her his card should she need anyone to talk to, but that she did not take up the offer.

Int: Did you find it easier to talk to women or men about your husband's death?

Ellie: Because my husband worked with men, I found it easier to talk to them, but there again, I did find it easy to talk to the women on my side of the family.

Int: Yes.

Ellie: And even one of Nick's work colleagues even wrote me a letter saying you know how sad he was and everything else. How Nick had helped him because he was in the services as well and he's seen some nasty things and him and Nick would talk, so yes, he helped other people.

In this exchange, it seems that Ellie found her husband's services connection made it easier to talk to men about her husband's death. The exceptions to this were the women in her own family. Ellie recalls one of Nick's work colleagues writing to say how her husband had helped him through some nasty times.

Int: Going back to loneliness, did you feel lonely afterwards or?

Ellie: Yes

Int: How did you cope with that?

Ellie: I tried to keep busy, and like I said, I was one that wrote the letters and everything. I went back to work as soon as I could.

The interviewer goes back to asking Ellie about how she coped with loneliness. Ellie reiterates her previous response by saying that she kept busy by writing letters and going back to work.

Int: How did you get there?

Ellie: I started off in a taxi then I had my car. So that was good.

Int: Did you take the person, your friend locally in the cab or just go on your own?

Ellie: I think my friend came as well and I used to give her a lift in when I got my little car, and if it was snowing, or I needed de-icing, my son used to get up before he went to college and de-ice the car for me.

Int: How kind.

Ellie affirms her travelling arrangements to work after Nick died and comments on how helpful her son was when it came to de-icing the car.

Int: Is there anything else you want to add?

Ellie: It was mainly family that stood by me, because friends either they're embarrassed or just didn't know how to handle it. I wasn't one of these people that burst into tears every two minutes. I was strong. I had to be strong because of my son. But yeah, I found that family really were there, but friends and that sort of dwindled away, particularly my best friend. I mean I invited her and her husband over for a coffee last year and then made arrangements and then at the last minute they said no, they'd changed their mind.

Int: That's hard, isn't it?

Ellie: It is

The interviewer asks the fairly typical 'anything else you want to add?' question and Ellie takes this as an opportunity to reiterate that her family stood by her and that despite the fact that she had to be 'strong' for her son and so was not prone to sudden tears her friends were either embarrassed or did not know how to handle her bereavement. Family, she says, were 'really there' but friends dwindled away, particularly her 'best friend'. The interviewer confirms how hard it is to cope with desertion by friends.

Int: So, would you think that there's a difference between loneliness and being alone?

Ellie: Yes

Int: How would you define that?

Ellie: Right. You can be in a crowded room with loads of people and still feel alone. But if you've got something to keep your mind occupied, you can still feel lonely.

Int: Yes.

Ellie: But it's the feeling alone to me is a back breaker. Because you feel as though there's nobody to help you, nobody there to rely on, to back you up if you're feeling down, but yeah, there you go. As I say, you can be in a crowded room but still feel lonely. Yes.

The interviewer, drawing on previous interview experience, asks Ellie if she sees a difference between loneliness and being alone. Ellie provides a succinct definition of the difference with which the interviewer simply agrees. This leads Ellie to go on to say that being alone is the back-breaker because you feel there is nobody to help you or rely on or will back you up. However, she reiterates you can still feel lonely in a crowded room.

Int: It's true. You said with loneliness you tried to keep busy, you went back to work, so, now you don't work. What happened that changed that?

Ellie: The MS I did start working from home which was good, but there again you can feel isolated. And when there's a meeting that's taking place your boss can't be bothered to phone you up and tell you what's going on that's not good. So then, with the MS, I suggested getting pensioned off. And the manager said, you won't be able to do that, it's too compli-cated, it's, it takes up too much time; and he was making all these excuses. So when I spoke to the lady from HR she said that was a load of rubbish and within about a month after speaking to her, I had been pensioned off.

The interviewer summarises some of Ellie's earlier comments and asks Ellie about her changing circumstances. Ellie talks about MS and the way in which thoughtless people can isolate those who work from home. As a consequence of this form of isolation Ellie requested retirement. While her line manager claimed that it was too complicated and made excuses, Ellie went straight to her employer's HR team where a woman told her that her line manager was talking a load of rubbish and within a month Ellie had retired.

Int: That's brilliant. How long ago was it that your husband died?

Ellie: He died – I've got it on a piece of paper. He died in 2007. He was only forty-three. I'd only known him to go to the doctors twice. We'd been married twenty years when he passed away and he was only forty-three. And if he was still here we'd have been married twenty-eight years. Yeah it was, people are always laughing, joking and even now Nick will say something and it's things like. It's like Yakult. You know the drink, Yakult.

Int: Yes

Ellie: And I said to Nick one time, I said you know why it's called Yakult don't you, and he said, tell me. I say 'cos it's yucky. And that has stuck. If ever we see the advert on the telly, Sam will say, it's called that because it's yucky and it was just, it's just silly little things that we, we used to do. The last holiday the three of us went down to London and that was lovely and we've got what we call our bridge.

Int: Which one's that?

Ellie: Tower Bridge, it's everybody's bridge, but if we see it on the telly it's there's our bridge. We planned to go abroad on holiday and we were planning on going abroad and we had booked London up for New Year. Of course, Nick died before that, so I had to cancel and that was, that wasn't nice. I've never like, we just went down to see my family instead and stayed with them and brought the New Year in, so yes.

Int: But hard.

Ellie: Yes, and again, pretty lonely. Because everywhere I mean it's like when you split up with a boyfriend or that you go to places you think, this where we used to go, we used to do this, and that's what it was like when I used to go anywhere, because Nick and I went everywhere. Even Sam was saying, we went there with dad, and here, there wasn't many places where we didn't go together. But yeah, we had good fun it was a good marriage.

Int: That's nice to have those happy memories.

The interviewer endorses Ellie's success in being able to retire and then changes the subject to ask how long it was since her husband died. This leads Ellie to first give the date when he died (edited to maintain anonymity) and secondly to begin to talk about her marriage to Nick. In doing so she goes on to recall the jokes they shared, the places they went to, and all the fun they had together. This confirms her capacity to remember the joy she had in Nick's company rather than the grief she felt at his death.

Ellie: Yes. I, Nick and I never really argued; he, I never saw him drunk, he never laid a finger on me, the only thing that wasn't good about him was that he smoked but as I say he didn't drink, he liked driving. I liked being the passenger, so yeah, it's like he liked the, he liked the red sweets and I didn't and I used to like black sweets and he didn't so we never used to argue over sweets.

Int: Bit like Jack Sprat

Ellie: Yeah, the things that, he liked, I would obviously give them to him and the things that he didn't like that I liked would obviously give to me. It was, we had a good marriage, it was really good, really good.

Ellie reiterates the good points about her marriage and the reasons why she felt they got on so well together by describing how they 'balanced' each other.

Int: Do you have now, more happy memories than sad memories?

Ellie: Yes.

Int: And when did that occur, or was it there from the start?

Ellie: It was there from the start, like I said, Nick was like my soul mate. We were always laughing. We were hardly ever in, and I, yeah, lots, lots of good memories. I can't really say, I can only remember one, one argument and was about, that was about money of all things you know. But no, that didn't amount to anything that was just an argument you know, finished with, get over it. Now it's my turn... yes. So, there you go.

Again Ellie emphasises the good points about her marriage stating that in twenty years of marriage they only ever had one argument. She describes Nick as her 'soul mate'.

Int: A difficult question, what did he die from?

Ellie: Heart attack

Int: Oh gosh

Ellie: It was a, this particular type of heart attack it apparently runs in his side of the family; he had clogging of the arteries and things like that. So Sam is checked by the doctor; the doctor was a really good support and help as well.

Int: That's good.

Ellie: Yes. When he found out Nick had passed away the doctor called me and asked me to go in and see him.

Int: That's good.

Ellie: So, I went in and then, because Nick had to have a post mortem, because his was a sudden death.

Int: Sudden death; yes.

Ellie: And the doctor called me in after he'd had the coroner's report and he talked me through it.

Int: That was kind.

Ellie: It is, if I had any questions I wanted to ask him, he even said to me, I'm going to prescribe you some sleeping pills because you know what it's like, you don't particularly sleep very well. He, I said no, no thank you, he said, he says, I'll give you the prescription, if you don't use them, don't use them, they're there if you need them.

Int: So, did you?

Ellie: No. No. It's like another easy thing was. Although my husband didn't really drink we have alcohol. I could quite easily have sat and drunk myself stupid at night, but I had a couple of drinks and I thought, no this is just too easy, to fall into this and just drink yourself stupid. So I came up with a plan, I'm never ever going to drink alone and to that day I have never drunk alone. But you don't have to get drunk to have a good time.

Int: No

Ellie: Or to forget about things.

Int: When you're not drunk?

Ellie: You've got to make more happy memories rather than dwelling on the past.

The interviewer asks Ellie how her husband died which leads Ellie to talk about the support her GP gave her and her family; how he talked through the Coroner's report with her; and offered her medication. He gave her a prescription for her to use if she needed it. Ellie goes on to say that she rejected the pills; she rejected alcohol as a solution to loneliness and spoke of the importance of making happy memories rather than 'dwelling on the past'.

Int: Was there a time when you felt that you'd come through something or was it a general process over the years?

Ellie: I think it was a process over the years, but that counselling really did help and that wasn't until Nick had been….

Int: Was the counselling your second year?

Ellie: Yeah and that really did help; it just; I mean I could smile before but not like I smiled after the counselling.

Int: It's interesting that you said that the first year, people assumed once you'd got through a year you'd be all right. Some said categorically not, a lot of people I've spoken to have said it went on.

Ellie: Yes. It does yeah.

Int: Second year, did you find it particularly hard?

Ellie: The anniversaries, yeah like wedding, birthday, his death, his funeral that sort of thing yeah. I mean we always celebrate now, not celebrate, but commemorate.

Int: Yes.

Ellie: And he was a, because Nick always liked a cup of tea, I drink coffee, but on his birthday, and the day he was cremated, we always have a cup of tea for Nick.

Int: That's nice

Ellie: And we sit out in the dining room table and we talk about him and we laugh and we have a cup of tea, that's good.

The interviewer re-opens the topic of counselling and Ellie simply reiterates how helpful it was. The interviewer then reports that people have told her that they are not 'all right' after the first year of bereavement; grief simply goes on. Ellie talks about anniversaries that her and her son like to commemorate.

Int: Do you feel that there is a part of you that's missing?

Ellie: Yes

Int: It's not gone away.

Ellie: Nope

Int: Do you think it ever will?

Ellie: No

Int: Why not?

Ellie: He was such a big part of my life, I loved him so much. He could be a pain in the back like any other man, but I loved him, yes. But yeah, we didn't Mick and I don't do the sort of things that Nick and I would have done.

Int: No

Ellie: I mean Mick's one of these people who'd rather sit in and watch telly but I'd rather be out you know, go for a drive or whatever. But yeah, there is still that big hole.

Int: A friend of mind, her husband died in 1997, she got re-married (deletion) she's very happy with person she's married, which is lovely, but it was just that she said this void never goes, which I thought was quite interesting.

Ellie: You learnt to, learn to live with the hurt that you have.

Int: You use the word hurt.

Ellie: Yeah. It's sort of you know you'll never see them again and can't talk to them again.

Int: Is that grief?

Ellie: That is, yeah, yeah. You learn to live with it, it doesn't get (sighs) you just learn to live with it, it's still there. I mean it's like I've got photographs on this side of the fridge of Nick and if I'm doing the dishes I don't if every picture's obviously apart from those, but yeah if I'm doing the dishes, washing my hands, whatever you know I can, I still talk to him.

Int: Yes

Ellie: Yep. Still talk to him. I still ask him things, doesn't answer me but. Yeah, men! But yeah.

Following a fairly abbreviated exchange, Ellie goes on to say that despite enjoying her current relationship there is still 'that big hole'. The interviewer offers a vignette of a friend in similar circumstances and Ellie says that you learn to live with the 'hurt'. She acknowledges that this 'hurt' is grief. She says that she still talks to Nick but he doesn't 'answer me'. Again, she exercises irony: 'Yeah! Men!'

Int: Are there particular things that he did in the home that struck you afterwards, now I've got to do these?

Ellie: He would like to tidy the garage. I mean that's like a, just a load of rubbish it was.

Int: I'm hoping right. O.K. sorry. Yeah

Ellie: Changing light bulbs. I mean that is now Sam's job, any things around the house that Nick would do. Sam likes to think that he's the man now he can do it and a lot of the time he can.

Int: Yes.

Ellie: A lot of the time he forgets but you know. But yeah, Sam's good, he's his dad all over again.

Int: Do you find that hard?

Ellie: I find that comforting. I think that is good. I mean it's like now, Sam if he's going out, he'll give me a kiss on the cheek.

Int: That's nice

Ellie: Yes. Or if I say you know, I feel a bit down today, he'll say right come on then mum, give us a hug. And you know a little hug, or just for no reason at all, we're in the kitchen and he'll either tap me on the back or I'll tap him and we just give each other a hug.

Int: That's nice

Ellie: Yeah

Ellie acknowledges that there were things that Nick 'always' did, but also says that these jobs have now become her son's. She also mentions the closeness of her relationship with her son, who is sensitive to when she is feeling a bit low by giving her a hug.

Int: Is there anything else you want to add?

Ellie: Apart from yes, I do miss him, I think about him every day. I also mention him in my prayers every night. I don't think there's a day go past that I don't think about him. And I mean that's what eight years ago now. But.

Int: Mention him in your prayers every night, have you got a religious background or affiliation?

Ellie: Not particularly. I started going but, when I was little when we lived in the North, we used to go to Sunday school. Then we moved down here, 'cos that's where my dad came from and church wasn't a priority. You know, weddings, funerals that sort of thing. Then, because my cousin used to go, go to the church in town and the youth club on the Friday night, I started going and the Reverend was, oh he was a lovely man, really, really, really nice. And I then said to my mum I want to get christened because my mum, my mother had my sister christened but not me. And I had a little brother at the time and I said he and I can get christened at the same time. So, we did.

But yeah, I mean I have, I mean when you're little, my mum would say you know say your prayers and go to sleep, that's what we used to do. So it my, my mum told me, oh when I was little you know, time for bed and I said, yeah, quick Jesus tender and then I'll go to sleep and that was the prayer you know. 'Jesus tender shepherd hear me, bless our little lamb tonight' so that was a quick Jesus tender then I'll go to sleep. But I, I pray every night and I ask God to look after Nick's soul and Tom and Liza, which was his mum and dad and my dad, to look after everybody.

Int: Yes.

Ellie: And I thank him for Sam because I'd had, there were about five miscarriages and we had Sam, that's five, but I've only got the one.

Int: That must have been really tough.

Ellie: That, that was tough, that got to the stage where I even said to Nick, why don't you go and find somebody that can give you family. But nope, he stuck with me, we had Sam so that's good. God's gift. Yes.

Int: That's lovely

Ellie: Yeah. So, as I say in my prayers I always thank him for Sam, ask him to keep Sam, his partner and their child safe, yeah. I don't, I like to think I am a Christian, don't go to church but I still pray and I'm a believer. There you go. That I think has actually helped with, getting over Nick as well.

Int: Yes, in what way?

Ellie: Again, having somebody to talk to, if you know what I mean.

Int: Yes, yeah.

Ellie: Somebody to vent your concerns and your fears and everything and also to provide a bit of hope.

The interviewer asks the standard closing question again and at this point Ellie incidentally reports that she mentions Nick in her prayers every night. As Ellie continues, the interviewer checks Ellie's religious background or affiliation. Ellie says that she has no particular affiliation; she reports a typical Anglican profile of 'weddings, funerals' etc. but then she goes to church with her cousin and joins the youth club and meets a priest who she describes as a 'lovely man'. She then tells her mum that she wants to be christened with her little brother. So, she acknowledges she has some religious affiliation and that every night she would pray before sleep. She says that she still prays asking God to look after the souls of departed relatives and to look after everybody. Then she gives thanks for Sam who she describes as 'God's gift'. She asks God to take care of her immediate family and keep them safe. She says that although she does not go to church she likes to think she is a 'Christian'. We note that Ellie prays for the souls of departed relatives and for the well-being of living relatives but not for herself. She also talks about the comfort of having God to talk to, listening to her concerns and fears and also providing hope and says how much this has helped her during her bereavement.

Int: Yes, is there anything else you want to say?

Ellie: You know who your true friends are when you're left alone.

Int: Yes

Ellie: Oh yes. It's like one of the most difficult things was, taking the wedding ring off. Though I didn't have to, but I've got Nick's wedding ring and my wedding ring inside Nick's wedding ring in a box in my jewellery box because I thought, we can't be together, but our rings can.

Int: Yes

Ellie: Yep

Int: A symbol of eternal love.

Ellie: That's right, both together. Just

Int: Thank you

Ellie: Thank you

The interviewer, yet again, asks the concluding question and this time Ellie observes that you know who your true friends are when you are alone. She then tells the Interviewer how she put Nick and her wedding rings together in a box which she agrees is a symbol of eternal love. It then appears the interview has concluded.

Int: Did you ever feel that people wanted to fix something for you?

Ellie: Yes, on the lonely side of things. Like double dating, and things like that which I mean, you can have a laugh and a giggle and go out with somebody but they don't have to pair you up with somebody. But yeah people do try and pair you up so that you're not lonely, sad, whatever. But that's just their thoughts. Not how you actually feel. Because sometimes it's nice to be alone, because then you can go over things in your mind you can think back, you can have a cry if you want to. But if it was somebody different, one they might not understand as much. It's still nice to talk things over with them but, you don't need pairing off. There you go.

Int: H'm. That's quite interesting. And, did you ever feel embarrassed when people tried to pair you off? Or suggest you ought not to be on your own?

Ellie: Yes, but there again, when you explain to them, you know, O.K. my husband's died, I'm alone, I've got to cope with that, before I move on. So, then they've got to deal with that as well. Don't try and push me into a relationship because if you go into a relationship you could end up hurt and that's not good.

Int: No

Ellie: No. There you go. Welcome

Int: Thank you.

When the interviewer switched the tape off, Ellie started talking about double dating and with her permission the interviewer re-started the interview. Ellie discusses the way others try to 'fix' her single situation by pairing her up with someone, so that she is not lonely or sad. Ellie sees that as a potential laugh or giggle but that actually it is their problem, not hers, because sometimes she likes to be alone and to think back; she concludes the interview.

WHAT DOES ELLIE TELL US ABOUT GRIEF?

Ellie's story is rather different from the others we have heard. By the time we were able to interview Ellie, her husband had been dead for eight years. Ellie has a longer term view of grief compared with some of the other people we interviewed. She talks about the initial impact of grief and speaks immediately of the importance of her family and especially her sister who was always there for her. Although the interviewer asked about people outside the family who helped her, she mentioned a few people, but always reverted to the help and support she had been given by her immediate family. She also talks about how 'others' assumed that once you had got through a year, you would be all right. However, Ellie is adamant that your grief goes on. She does tell us that she and her son commemorate him with good memories and laughter. She also talks about the hurt of knowing you will never see them again and will not be able to talk with them again, and that that is the grief that you learn to live with because it is still there. There is still 'that big hole'.

DEATH OF A LOVED ONE; FUNERAL ARRANGEMENTS; KEEPING BUSY; ANNIVERSARIES:

In talking about Nick's death, it is not until nearly the end of the interview that she mentions that he died from a heart attack in the night. She talks about the help and support her doctor gave her in explaining the Coroner's report and also about the minister who conducted the service thoughtfully, and who gave her his card so that she could ring him if she needed extra support. She says that she found him approachable. She also talks about how helpful the funeral directors were, particularly with the booklet they gave her as it enabled her to deal with some of the practicalities of death. However, she talks at length about keeping busy with dealing with the practicalities of Nick's death and in writing letters. She was also working at the time, which again kept her busy. Through keeping busy, she is able to keep her grief at bay, but acknowledges that her sister was always there for her should she need a good cry. She tells us that there were four people who were closely involved in comforting her and helping with the funeral arrangements: her sister, her son and Nick's parents. Involving her son in the funeral arrangements has meant her keeping Nick's ashes for the time until her son wants to scatter them. She talks a lot about working as a family 'team', which is important for her, which included Nick's parents. Although Ellie has a new partner, Nick is still part of her life and she and her son still commemorate his birthday and the day he was cremated by having a cup of tea round the dining table, even though she, herself, is a coffee drinker. It was Nick who was the tea-drinker.

CONTRASTING FRIENDS AND FAMILY:

Even though the interviewer asks about people who helped her outside the family, Ellie immediately talks about her sister, who was her supportive backbone at the time of Nick's death. She was there for advice, comfort and shared Ellie's grief. She speaks of her family 'team' which clearly includes her son. She found that her family were 'really there'. At the time of bereavement, Nick's mum and dad were supporting Ellie and equally, Ellie found herself supporting them. We felt that there was a real sense of sadness that friends, particularly her best friend, sort of dwindled away. Although she was able to talk to a couple of her work colleagues, others did not know what to say and, in Ellie's words, just kept 'shtum'.

AN APPRECIATION OF COUNSELLING:

The interviewer brings up the topic of being lonely and it is at this point that Ellie talks about receiving counselling, which initially she was not very keen on, but then acknowledges that it was the best thing she could have done, as she was able to 'smile' again at the end of it. The counsellor was a woman, who was not perturbed by Ellie bursting into tears. She was just there to listen and was genuinely interested in what Ellie had to say. The counsellor made no attempt to force any opinion on her: she was just there 'listening'. Ellie reiterated how by having somebody who was 'there' and 'listened', and did not make any judgements, made her 'smile again', but she could not say exactly how the counsellor made this happen. She says that the counselling was good and that she would recommend it to anybody.

THE CONSTELLATION OF HER FAITH:

At the interviewer's second prompt to anything else Ellie would like to add, Ellie mentions that she prays for Nick every night. This then leads to Ellie talking about her faith and how important it is to her, even though she does not manifest this by going to a church. She reiterates that she has some religious affiliation and that it is very important for her to pray for the souls of Nick and departed relatives as well as praying for the well-being of her immediate family. However, she does not pray for herself. Superficially, Ellie would appear like many others who attend births, weddings and funerals; however, when she talks about the inspirational priest of her teenage years, it becomes apparent that she has a deep faith, which she has found very helpful as she feels she is able to talk to God about what is troubling her, as well as to be thankful to Him for her son, his partner and their child, and the good things in her life. She also says how much she found having a faith helped her 'get over' Nick. She sees God as providing a bit of hope.

SOME DISCURSIVE POINTS:

A) IRONY:

It seemed to us that Ellie used irony on a number of occasions in the interview. On the first occasion, she observes that it seemed as if her best friend stepped back as though if Ellie could not help her, she would not help Ellie. Ellie observes 'that's a good best friend, isn't it?' Here the usage seems rather rueful. The other two usages seem rather happier. In one, she talks about Sam as 'her little boy who's all grown up now', and in the second Ellie remarks that she still talks to Nick. She still asks him things but he does not answer, to which she adds, 'Yeah, men!' Here she seems to be laughing about men, but also laughing about herself.

B) BEING ALONE AND BEING LONELY:

Drawing on experience, the interviewer asks Ellie if she sees any difference between being lonely and alone. Ellie replies by talking about counselling and a later prompt about loneliness led to Ellie talking about being busy. The interviewer then asks if there is a difference between loneliness and being alone. Ellie then responds by saying that being alone is a 'backbreaker' and that you have to cope, that there is no one there to help you, no one to rely on and no one to back you up when you are feeling down. She also adds that it can be nice to be alone as you then have time to think, and time to cry, and that you know who your true friends are when you are left alone. Ellie talks about those people who wanted to 'fix' it so that she had a partner, and that some of her friends arranged a double date for her. However, she felt that this was 'their' problem as she did not want to be pushed into a relationship. She says that you can be lonely in a crowded room.

C) GENDER:

Ellie reports two significant women who helped: her sister and her counsellor. She also talks about the importance of Nick working in the armed services and a colleague of her husband wrote to Ellie to tell her how Nick had helped him through some nasty times. Ellie says that this services' contact made it easy for her to talk to men, although the only ones named were the undertaker, the doctor and the minister, along with two men who her husband used to work with. It is unusual that it was male managers who would pop in to see her.

11

IAN'S STORY

INTERVIEW WITH IAN WITH EMBEDDED COMMENTARY

Int: Talk your way through what happened after Geraldine died, especially about those people outside your family who helped.

Ian: Who helped.... I'm the wrong person to ask really. I... being medically trained, you... you think you're prepared for all these things. I was anticipating Geraldine's death. I thought she might die two or three years before and then therefore, had plenty of time to get used to it. I think ordinary people help in lots of ways. I remember my first wife died, the thing that actually helped me. It sounds totally ridiculous, we had a bunch of drinking Irish in the pub and for six months at least, if not a year, if I moved towards the bar, these big fellas just moved out the way. It... it honestly just as a matter of respect, whereas before they would have just ignored it.

Int: How nice.

Ian: Yeah, it was it was, it was absolutely charming.

Int: Oh that's lovely, yeah, oh..

Ian: Just stupid little things..

WE NOTE THAT Ian had hoped to have time to prepare for Geraldine's death and that he thinks ordinary people help in lots of ways. The anecdote he uses to illustrate this is labelled confusingly 'ridiculous, absolutely charming and stupid'. It relates to his first wife's death. We suggest that these conflicting adjectives describe Ian's sense of being touched, yet at the same time being embarrassed at something that might appear to be trivial in the eyes of others.

Int: Are there any other little bits and pieces you remember?

Ian: I was surprised at Geraldine's little wake. How the number of people that were there and the...the amount of sympathy that was obvious, you didn't need to ask for it.

Int: What did they say?

Ian: We're blokes. You don't say things do you, you minimise what you say. It's not in what you say it's what you do.

Int: So, what did they do?

Ian: Nothing..little..little things. It's a... silly little things. I...I meant... I genuinely meant that about the pub. It was a mark of respect they wouldn't..wouldn't insult you by buying you drinks.

Int: No.

Ian: But they made it absolutely plain that you had the right to get one there and then. You didn't have to wait (laughs)

Int: Didn't have to wait, you come first.

Ian: Yes..yes..lovely blokes.

Ian re-visits his pub narrative (again a silly little thing) but on this occasion, it illustrates what Ian believes to be a gender specific trait. He says 'We're blokes' and goes on to elaborate what he feels to be masculine behaviour. 'It's not what you say, it's what you do'.

Int: And with Geraldine, what sort of practical help did you have?

Ian: The bit that mattered was the palliative care team, just before she died. The same with my mother and I'm very sad they've been downgraded yet again.

Int: Which palliative?

Ian: Well it was team for the whole area and they were fighting for survival at the time when Geraldine was ill. They'd already been half strengthened before, I think before they were all registered nurses, by the time they came here they were half and half.

Int: O.K.

Ian: No the biggest issue was, being able to deal with incontinence.

Int: Yes, that's hard.

Ian: Once I knew the ladies would pop in every four hours then that was dealt with.

Int: And that's a very private thing isn't it.

Ian: I didn't have to do it for her. They did it for me.

We have edited some of the very graphic description which underlined how important palliative care was to Ian.

> Int: *Were there any special people, the fellows in the pub, special people after Geraldine died, who particularly helped you, or were particularly sympathetic, empathetic?*
>
> Ian: *Well when one has a wide circle of acquaintances or one did, and a limited number of friends, or true friends, but no, they were, there were a few people round the club that were over, you know they would have listened..they..if I'd wanted to talk.*
>
> Int: *Yes.*
>
> Ian: *Which I think is what really, people really need.*
>
> Int: *Need to listen.*

Ian acknowledges that he knew that there would always be a listening ear if he had needed one, and that that is what he thinks people really need.

> Ian: *When Prudence died, I, I knew a child psychiatrist and I, he was a nice, very superficially cynical gentleman, very wise, and I, after a meeting I cornered him quietly and said, what shall I do about the children and he said, just talk, just talk, and, and look for help if you think you've got problems. Don't rush into counselling, don't rush into this, that and the other.*

Ian's perspective on listening is illustrated by an anecdote related to the death of his first wife. The advice he received was to talk and talk and to look for help if he thought his children had problems which implies listening carefully to what his children said.

> Int: *What is it about listening that's so important?*

Ian: Well it's really listening, isn't it? It's actually, not using the conversation as a way of getting across your point of view, actually listening to what somebody's saying, then trying to, just give them time. I mean so many people, like most counselling, yeah, if you talk enough you find your own solutions.

Ian recognises that talking can be a way of making a point without actually listening to what the other is saying. The second point Ian makes is that many people, given enough space to talk, will find their own solutions.

Int: An organisation I know of always advises the most important thing is to listen, never offer advice.

Ian: But you can have three people that listen and two of them aren't really listening at all, they're just waiting for an opportunity to get their point of view over. I tend to be like that now (laughs)

Int: I can on occasions

Ian: ......don't just listen, hear.

Ian offers an analysis of conversation where there is no real exchange, rather a cue to add a point of view and from here he goes on to suggest that beyond listening is the importance of hearing what is said.

Int: Who are the people who listened most and you found most helpful?

Ian: The biggest help I've had was my youngest. If I'm totally honest, that was over the whole thing......has always been insightful, always been very clever, play plays down how bright s/he is.

Ian talks about how the youngest member of his immediate family had so much insight and was so helpful.

Int: Anybody outside the family?

Ian: In little ways yes, lots, lots of people but no, nobody specific. I say don't forget, I'm a medical person.

Int: I do appreciate that.

Ian: I know, what, what really hit me when Prudence died more than Geraldine, was how unprepared emotionally I was for the event. I mean she, she died, within twelve hours …… or something like that, and that was, one minute we're there, the next minute we're somewhere else. And I thought I was prepared for anything you know, I'd been in casualty, you'd been, you'd seen people die all the time, often questionably unnecessarily and then all of a sudden something happens and you've got a huge hole in your life.

Int: Mm.

What Ian tells us is that although he is a medical person and has seen all sorts of things in casualty and saw himself as prepared for anything, he was not prepared for the death of his first wife which left a 'huge hole' in his life.

Ian: The biggest help were the children.

Int: I was going to say how did you cope?

Ian: Yeah that was the focus.

Int: Yes.

Ian: And my parents.

Int: What did the children do that helped?

Ian: They, they had to be looked after. I couldn't sit down and mope. I had to get on. I also had to work. I had to make money to look after them.

Int: And so?

Ian: And so that closed down all sorts of other avenues and just concentrate on them.

Int: Yes

Here Ian tells us that his children helped him cope because he had to take care of them and to earn money to provide for them. Ian also mentions that his parents were invaluable in helping too.

Ian: ….The bigger loss was ten years later when they left, left home. I had the empty nest syndrome when my youngest was eighteen, when s/he went to university.

Int: Yes, that must have been hard.

Ian: It was hard, for twelve years, because you, mean know what it's like, you, you get six weeks of doing exactly what you want and you just get into one routine and then it's thrown upside down again and you get the other routine and you like both of them, but you have to adjust each time and it's, and, and in a way that's kind of the nature of (life)? I actually think divorce is a worse bereavement for people than, than death. Because you don't get any public sympathy and you've got all the sense of loss and shame and did I do enough, or what did I do wrong.

This sounds as if Ian is reflecting on his experience with his children. This leads him to say that it is better to be widowed than to be divorced. The shame Ian links to divorce may seem rather alien to contemporary readers. We see it as an indicator of a very strong value system.

> *Int: You almost touched on it, being bereaved, loneliness. Prudence had children, but how did you feel with Geraldine dying, lonely afterwards?*

> *Ian: Yes, in a sense, yes of course. It wasn't just that I was confounded by the events, but over the previous seven years, dad and mum had died and in a kind of way dad had become my best friend over many years. We sort of shifted from being father and son to getting on very well together, gradually over a number of years. I mean I actually kissed him for the first time about three or four weeks before he died.*

The interviewer prompts with a question about the loss of two life partners. Ian chooses to speak of the death of his parents and in particular the loss of his father with whom he felt he had found a new best friend.

> *Int: Oh, how lovely.*

> *Ian: Surprisingly, he didn't reject it (laughs)*

> *Int: Obviously the relationship was very good.*

> *Ian: He was a marvellous man.*

> *Int: Yes*

> *Ian: You know they talk about silver spoons in life, but to have two very ordinary parents that just like you, ha! Is the real silver spoon.*

> *Int: Lovely*

Ian:I found, I found mother tearing up letters he'd written to her during the war and I told her off. I said you don't want to do that. She said, 'I've read them. I shall remember' and there were things in there about me when I was tiny. The sun shone out of my backside – that was him writing to her (laughing), there's never been another baby like Ian. (laughing)

For a little while there is just Ian speaking about his father in a slightly fragmented manner until his final reflections upon both his parents, with just brief interlocutions from the interviewer. By referring to a silver spoon, Ian is speaking of a sense of wealth – in this case two wonderful parents. His recollections of his mother destroying his father's war time letters, transport Ian to a time where his parents thought he was perfect. He expresses these events and feelings in a very traditional way and we suspect with some embarrassment indicated by his laughter.

Int: Nice. How do you cope with being on your own now?

Ian:I'm not unhappy in my own company. I never have been. No, I think the bigger worry is if anything goes wrong. I mean about a month after Geraldine died, I had gastric bleeding.........and it took months to build it up again and I felt incredibly vulnerable. You suddenly think if anything goes wrong, I, I'm on my Jack, mate.

Int: Yes, yeah

Ian:But I think you can be in marriage anyway. I mean I know enough marriages where in fact they co-exist but they wouldn't support each other when (laughing) not for very long anyway.

Ian is not lonely; he is happy in his own company and says he always has been. However, he acknowledges that if there are any difficulties in his life he

is alone. (I'm on my Jack). Here he is making the distinction between being
lonely and being alone.

*Int: Geraldine had a sort of religious funeral. Was there any help from
any church?*

*Ian:No. I, I know if I'm being honest I, I think she was, I'm not quite
sure what, what I think she...We as kids we mixed round across between
the Church of England the, the Brethren. Geraldine I think was Church
of England, and I think it's Baptists she went to, but I think she lost all
religious associations.*

Int: So had no church connections at all?

Ian:No, no.

Int: O.K.

Ian:No, in fact it was, no, no, no. No generally not.

Int: O.K.

*Ian:I, I must be honest. I mean when, when I was a teenager, I wouldn't
be confirmed. I toyed with the idea, I even went to Bible class at the
Hall, and I was very into it.*

Ian provides us with some brief observations on their religious affiliations as a youngster, but referring to their current circumstances, says
that they had no church connections. He says 'No' seven times in this
conversations.

The telephone rang and the recording was turned off for a few minutes.

Int: Do you find it easier to talk to women or men about Geraldine or Prudence?

Ian: Don't, never discussed it much with either.

Int: O.K.

Ian: It, it's different. I mean some of the blokes in the pub have asked quietly how, you, it, but you know what men are like. It's at a much more gentle level, 'you alright mate?' and, also inquiring about things, almost to wonder how they'd feel if the same happened to them.

Int: Yeah.

Ian: But there?

Int: What do women do then that are different?

Ian: I haven't got that many women the, who, who are close enough. There are a few in the pub that I know and they avoid the topic, you know, you know the emotional support is there if you wanted to cry on their shoulder you could, but, I've not felt the need to do that.

Ian tells us he has not talked about his bereavements much with either men or women. He tells us how some men at the pub ask quietly at a much more gentle level (although not explicit) he might be contrasting this gentleness with male 'loudness' or the more 'immediate' support that women potentially offer ('if you wanted a shoulder to cry on').

Int: It's O.K. Is there anything else you'd like to add?

Ian: It's only going back to what I, I was saying when I was in-terrupted. I, I really did take Christianity very seriously when I was a kid. I agonised about it. I, I very nearly became confirmed into the Church of England and baulked because I genuinely didn't think I could live up to the principles of the religion. And I think it's medicine. I saw too many things happen to nice people, that when Prudence died I bemoaned fate but I was so glad I wasn't ap-pealing to a divine God to do something different because I, I just couldn't believe in it. It actually made it easier. Cos that was fate, isn't it? Otherwise besides which, all my mates would be down in hell. I don't want to be up in heaven singing praises to a divine God when I, I could sit with them (laughing)

The interviewer asks the standard closing question. Ian returns to his view of Christianity as a youth and his rejection of the Church of England because he did not think he could live up to the principles of the religion and then, as a result of his career in the health service, where too many bad things can happen to nice people, he found it difficult to appeal to a divine God to change things. Following this rather profound intellectual observation, he then counterpoints this with a fairly old joke about looking forward to a good time with his mates down in hell.

Int: Point taken!

Ian: Sorry.

Int: No, no that's absolutely fine. Is there anything else you want to add?

Ian: No, no, no.

Int: All right. O.K. Thank you.

The interviewer reiterates the closing question and gets an emphatic three 'No's' in response.

WHAT DOES IAN TELL US ABOUT GRIEF?

It is difficult to know how to interpret Ian's silence on grief and grieving, and his capacity to glide away from such questions. He readily acknowledges how unprepared emotionally he was for the deaths of both his partners. Ian had thought himself prepared for anything; he had often seen people die, but in personal terms he speaks of a huge 'hole in your life'. He found that caring for others helped alleviate or avoid his grief. He describes in a somewhat derogatory fashion that sitting around moping was not a possibility.

BEING BUSY:

For Ian, a principle coping strategy for his multiple bereavements he speaks of (his parents and both wives) is to keep busy. Although he does not acknowledge this as a coping strategy, he does say that the biggest help were his children who needed to 'be looked after' and the same thinking applied to caring for his parents. He is also concerned about how best to care for his children. He found his youngest child his biggest single help.

THE DIFFERENCE BETWEEN BEING LONELY AND ALONE:

We ask Ian directly about how he copes with being on his own and he tells us that he is not unhappy in his own company and that he never has been, but he acknowledges he could feel incredibly vulnerable and speaks of sudden thoughts that if anything goes wrong he is on his own. So here Ian is being specific about the difference between being lonely and being alone. Elsewhere in the interview, he suggests that it is quite possible to be lonely even when one is married and co-habiting.

THE IMPORTANCE OF FAMILY:

We have already recognised the importance to Ian that his children are to him. Firstly, of course, in terms of keeping 'busy', but secondly in being there to support and comfort him in later life. Ian still talks of his parents in rather formal terms (mother/father). Initially they were supportive in helping him cope and then he had the challenge of taking care of them. He holds his late parents in great affection, speaking of them as the silver spoons he was born with and here he is not referring to material wealth but to the love and affection that was spent on him. He clearly felt that as a child he was cherished.

GENDER:

Ordinary people who help seem to be men, for example 'big fellas' who quietly made way for him. He saw this as a mark of respect. Nothing needed to be said because 'blokes' minimise what they say: it is what they do that is more important for Ian. Similarly, after his second wife died, men in the pub would discreetly ask if he was all right, but would not elaborate much further. He says he never discussed bereavement with either men or women. Some 'blokes' asked gently and he does not have that many women who he felt close enough with to discuss his bereavement. Although he was confident that the women he knew would provide emotional support or a shoulder to cry on 'had he felt the need for it'. From this we deduce that if he was going to expose his grief to anybody it would have been women.

SUPPORT FROM THE CHURCH:

Ian is ambivalent about his faith connections. Although the celebrant at Geraldine's funeral had a religious connection, Ian was not aware of Geraldine having any specific contact with a church in adult life. However, he speaks of their life as children mixing between the Church of England, the Brethren and the Baptists. As a youngster Ian took Christianity very seriously. He says he 'agonised' about it and nearly became confirmed into the Church of England. He 'baulked' because he genuinely believed he could not live up to the principles of the religion. He goes on to say that working in health care, he found it difficult to appeal to a divine God, when surrounded by so much suffering.

SOME UNIQUE DISCURSIVE FEATURES:

For us an underlying thread through Ian's conversation was his capacity to make light of some very genuine insights. The quiet male response to bereavement is described as 'helpful' and 'totally ridiculous' and absolutely 'charming' and 'stupid little things'. A mark of respect was seen as nothing – 'silly little things'.

Acknowledgement of masculine appreciation of his circumstances is almost simultaneously valued and devalued. Ian provides a rather moving vignette of his mother destroying his father's letters and he remembers how he was described in childhood, which he follows with a laughing comment 'the sunshine shone out of my backside' and laughing again, that there had never been 'a baby like Ian'.

In describing subtle differences between being lonely and being alone, Ian caps off his remarks with a laughing use of rhyming slang (Jack – Jones – alone)

In his closing remarks, Ian offers some very thoughtful observations about the challenge of meeting the high standards he saw in the Anglican tradition when surrounded by the suffering he saw in the health service. Having suggested that not having a faith and being able to appeal to a divine God, might make life easier, he closes these remarks with a rather hoary joke about wanting to join all his mates in hell when the time came.

In response to the interviewer's questions about religious affiliations, Ian offers an emphatic 'No' repeated twice and then in response to the interviewer's acceptance of this, he then repeats it five times, adding 'in fact' and 'generally not' to the mix. This appears to us to be an exceptionally strong rejection of all religious ties.

12

MAY'S STORY

INTERVIEW WITH MAY WITH EMBEDDED COMMENTARY

Int: Talk your way through what happened after Phillip died, those people outside the family who helped you most during those difficult days

May: After he died, do you mean the moment he died or do you mean after the funeral?

Int: After he died, I suppose the moments he died and afterwards.

May: Well first and foremost is that I had tremendous support from my husband so, in terms of a death, it was probably as good as we could get. So everything about a terrible experience had a lot of positivity – support, love, care, whatever you want to call it, so. It wasn't, although it was shocking, it wasn't a shock, because we had been prepared for it.

MAY ACKNOWLEDGES THAT although both she and her husband were in a 'terrible' situation, there was positivity in it all because they were able to support each other. It was not one-sided. They had both been prepared for the fact that he was not going to live, hence although it was 'shocking' it was not a 'shock'.

So, funeral director excellent, – family obviously very supportive, – and so you're meaning family and you're meaning friends and colleagues and such. Well Phillip's work place excellent – support for him and excellent for me as well. They were in touch – they rang me. The thing that I did find about it was that people..the thing I found really quite astonishing was how many people were able to come and talk to me as..I felt that people were very grown up, which I know sounds a bit ridiculous, but, people didn't, I didn't feel that people avoided me.

May talks about the people who were very supportive to both her and Phillip and lists them. What she most appreciated was the way in which people were able to come and talk to her and that they did not 'avoid' her.

Int: That's good.

May: Yeah, no, it was, it's fantastic. My son was living with me for the first year and immediately I, well I was already on, it wasn't compassionate leave, I was on long term sick leave. So, I started long term sick leave in the Autumn and Phillip died in the Autumn and so then I was due to go back to work in the, as it turned out, mid Spring. So, I was not working but I was supported by my place of work, by my immediate colleagues but also by my place of work in terms of cards, and flowers, but also, what are those food boxes called, you know those organic food boxes turned up as well which was a bit of a shock.

The interviewer gives a light weight prompt before May goes on to elaborate further. She talks about how her place of work allowed her to have as much leave as she wanted. Her colleagues were equally supportive not only through sending her flowers and cards but also by organising food boxes.

Int: Oh, how nice

May: Yes, (laughing). But so many people had been supporting Phillip through that process as well as myself that that pretty much continued you know people. Can I name names?

May is saying that the kind of support that she received whilst Phillip was so ill continued after he died and asks if it would be appropriate to name names.

Int: Yes of course you can

May: Well people like the ministers, (one female minister, one male and his wife who were also family friends – field notes) were tremendous support, as was Lyn. (four church goers – field notes). You know lots of friends, Cyril was a brilliant support, Annette and Pete, so people weren't hesitant and so many cards and letters and the letters weren't ..People had clearly spent time saying, oh I don't know, I hesitate the use..the word..the right thing, but it is astonishing when people write things that are so heart felt. No, I was very supported and so was Phillip but I know you've asked the question about after he died, but it it isn't actually either or

Int: No.

May: It goes together so there you go, is that the answer?

May lists four church goers and three others who were of exceptional support to her. In passing we note that there were four women and three men. May also valued the heartfelt messages on the cards she received. She then reiterates that although the interviewer is asking about events after Phillip's death, she does not see it that way. Rather she acknowledges a continuum of support.

Int: Can you remember what those people who supported you most said or did that made that special difference, empathy, sympathy, practical support. Still being supported by those people?

May: What can I remember, yes, physically we had food. Joan certainly in the last weeks of Phillip's life. Joan was providing food on a fairly regular basis I now remember. I'll never be able to look at pesto pasta again without thinking of that time, but more than happy to think about it, it was fine. I think it was people phoning, we had a lot of visitors we had lots of people visiting and that didn't stop and I think that takes enormous courage to turn up at somebody's house or to phone. So on, from their point of view I really admired all those people who never let, let me go. People didn't avoid it or me. What was the question?

May talks about the sort of support she received, which was food 'on a regular basis', people telephoning, and others who visited, which she appreciates must have required a tremendous amount of 'courage'. May, in retrospect, really admired 'people who never let me go'. They did not avoid her.

Int: Can you remember what those people who supported you most said or did that made that special difference?

May: But because Phillip's illness was such that we, what we had said way back when we discovered the diagnosis and we knew that the diagnosis had potentially oh a rubbish outcome which in, indeed it did. The one thing we started with, the one basis was it had to be the truth, we wouldn't do this in any other way except the truth so we had to have honesty. So we had talked to people all the way through, oh we didn't talk about death and dying and cancer all the time, we talked about normal things, and the price of milk and one of my neighbours, bless them, when Phillip was very poorly, knocked on the door and wanted, asked if we'd got some olive oil or something like that and it was so wonderful to be normal. But they didn't know he was ill and after he died they were just mortified and they said, well we would never have knocked on the door if we'd known. It's like, no, no, no, that's the whole point, we want you to knock on the door, we want you to treat us as if we're normal people because we still are even though we were in this terrible set of circumstances.

It was talking, it was people grieving with us, because people had lost a friend or a colleague. So, they needed to talk as well. So, empathy in the sense that they were going through it too, not empathising because they were empathising cos they'd had a death, they were grieving because they were grieving for Phillip. So,, friend or family I'm afraid I can't, I can't leave the family out of it.

The interviewer re-states the core question. May states that at the heart of all this support was not only being honest between herself and Phillip, but also about being honest with friends and neighbours about Phillip's ill health. This then led to both her and Phillip being able to 'normalise' a terrible situation. They were able to talk about general things and this led to their friends being able to take up the cue and follow suit. Although some said they would never have knocked if they had known, for May the whole point was wanting to be treated as normal. As a result of this May felt that people were grieving with them. Empathy here is defined by May as people 'going through the same thing too', not empathising because they too had known a death, but grieving for Phillip. In conclusion May reiterates the importance of family for her.

Int: Still being supported by those people?

May: Yes

Int: Being bereaved can mean loneliness, were you helped in any way to be able to come to terms with being on your own?

May: Can we stop for two seconds while I think, cos it could be more than two seconds while the thinking process goes on about that one.

Int: Absolutely fine.

(Break)

Int: Going to go on now, O.K.?

May: O.K. loneliness and being alone. I have said and I've said to (minister's name), on a number of occasions. There's a big difference between being lonely and being alone and I think that as a person I am very content in my own company so I don't feel loneliness particularly, however I do believe alone for myself is a much greater issue and it's not being alone because I'm rattling round the house on my own. It's being alone in terms of decision making and dealing with either big things, or tiny wee, little tiny things that really upset you. So, I, it wasn't loneliness and it isn't loneliness. The issue I think is and again, it's been discussed before, it's the opportunity to talk to other people when you need to talk to them, which may be quite late at night or at an awkward time in the afternoon or just before you go somewhere in the morning or just after you've walked the dog and you've got in the house and you've had a row with somebody on the walk and you need to talk to someone. It's that sort of alone when you need to talk something through. So I've been very fortunate because one of the ministers (female – field notes) lives very close and I do know there was a famous occasion when I went round in my jim-jams and slippers (laughs). But isn't that the point?

Int: Yes

May: Isn't that the point that that being feeling confident and comfortable, not confident enough, comfortable enough to be able to knock on a door which you wouldn't do if your other half was there because you wouldn't you would have that conversation and discussion with that person with you. And of course, sometimes the conversation isn't for your children, not that I have rows with my children particularly but sometimes you need to talk to someone of your own age to get an idea (laughing) oh dear. So, loneliness, no, no, I but alone I've had to get to grips with doing things on my own and that's tricky.

Following a brief unrecorded conversation, May sets out to contrast loneliness and being along. She says that as a person she is content in her own company, so does not feel loneliness. She feels that living alone means being alone in terms of decision making and dealing with everything from big things to small things that are distressing. For May being alone is missing the opportunity to talk to other people when you need to talk to them, albeit that time might not be very convenient for others. She recognises that being alone is not having somebody to talk things through with. For May, that was always her husband. Now she finds the antidote to loneliness (through loss of a life partner) is feeling confident and comfortable enough in your approach to another. That other needs to be somebody of about her own age, who will 'get an idea'. So, although on good terms with her children, May recognises the value of having somebody with whom she shares a mutual frame of reference. For May, getting 'to grips' with doing things on her own is quite distinct from loneliness.

Int: Are you still being helped in this?

May: Yes, yes of course I am, of course but and I have to say it's not just the minister, though she is excellent about this so..I would say that I don't, this is on the same point, but I have always talked about Phillip. I have never shied away from talking about him, I have never not mentioned him, and I think, I hope, I suspect that my friends and colleagues know that that's what I'm going to say. But I don't think that, but you know I might be wrong, I don't think I harp on about him. I think I felt very strongly at the beginning in the first few months actually I did feel it very, very strongly, that everything I did was in direct relation to him, either as a response of his death, or as a response of what I had to do and he wasn't here because I had to flipping do it now and he wasn't there to do it. And I felt very much, and I am going to cry now, I felt very much that he was the centre and I was all to..

The first sentence comprises four statements of her willingness to talk about Phillip.

Whilst May did not think Phillip was her only focus, she did recognise the first few months after Phillip's death were characterised by either responding to his death or to his absence and that there were many things she had to do on her own because Phillip was not there and he was her centre.

Int: Do you want me to stop? (May shakes her head – field notes). You sure?

May: No I'm certain. Unless you can't hear. No, no I'm fine.

Int: No, I'm happy to stop if you want. I know Phillip had a religious funeral, are you able to talk about the sort of support the church gave you or didn't give you?

May: That's an interesting one, because do you want to just stop that for a second now?

In an episode that characterises some of the emotional work of data gathering, the interviewer immediately checks that May is comfortable with the interview. She then cautiously begins asking about the support available from the church. May identifies this is an important point and asks for a break in the recording.

(Break)

Int: O.K. Yep we are back on.

May: Yes, yes, faith, faith was very important I felt, I felt Phillip's faith strengthened hugely and so did mine. I never felt unsupported by my faith. I never questioned it. I, whether, well maybe that is blind faith, who knows. I had tremendous support from people at the local church, tremendous support, because that was the church that we had been to most and where, where the funeral was, a tremendous support, again people were not shy. I have to mention the minister at the church and his wife. I have to mention Lyn. I have to mention the local female minister although she wasn't at our church. All of the congregation.

(Field note: Four lines breaching anonymity deleted)

May: Phillip and the minister (male – field notes) had been good friends and their, their friendship deepened enormously. And in the, in the summer, Phillip and I went to another church with the minister and his wife and that was very, very, very, very good. But to all intents and purposes we weren't going to church in the period to his death but we were still fully accepted as members there and since his death I have been going to a Cathedral which I found wonderful. The church support was tremendous even though we weren't officially members of the church because we'd not been going there for a little while but for no falling out or anything like that, just family life that was all. That was all. But, no, good, and what was the answer was, the question was are you still getting support?

May speaks of the importance of her faith to her and how her and Phillip's faith were strengthened. She acknowledges the support she got from the church where Phillip's funeral was held and again her appreciation of people's openness. In relation to this church, she acknowledges the support of a male minister, a female minister and two other women. She then goes on to speak of the deepening of Phillip's friendship with the male minister and reports a couple of months when she and Phillip went to another local church. She is emphatic about how good that was. She remarks although they were not attending regularly they still felt accepted as members. May compares their involvement with two different churches as being similar to family life. In passing, she tells us that she has found going to the Cathedral 'wonderful' and then she seeks a prompt from the interviewer as to what the question was about.

Int: It's are you able to talk about the sort of support the church gave you or didn't give you.

May: Well the support was, was extremely practical. But also, you just knew that if you'd asked for anything it would have been there. I remember going to the church to discuss the music with the musician and her husband and it was all when, when can you turn up May. It wasn't about when they could turn up, um. And you know the tea at the church was all just dealt with, just done and I remember talking to Lyn and saying you know if I give you money can that be, can that be resolved and I don't know if I gave them any money or not, I don't know if they refused the money, I can't remember, because I can't remember. I did offer money (laughs) I must have paid for what was required to be paid for, but we're not talking about that, no and, and I my, my feeling because you're in that blur is that all the stops were pulled out by the congregation for that funeral. That's my feeling that's how I think what happened, happened.

May talks about the practical support that was offered at the time of Phillip's death in organising the funeral. She is very appreciative of the way in which members of the congregation matched their availability with her needs. She then talks about whether or not she paid for the funeral tea, and then goes on to say that she knew she had paid for everything that needed to be paid for as regards the funeral itself. She acknowledges that that was not the focus of the question and that although her memory is a 'blur' she knows that the congregation pulled out all the 'stops' for Phillip's funeral.

Int: Congregation, what about clergy

May: Well it was the ministers (field note – delete five lines). They were the clergy. Yes, that's right and so, the minister, but, you know people like Tom and Dan.

Int: What did they actually do which helped?

May: I don't know they just were, they were just there.

Int: O.K.

May: Well just, I mean the minister, the minister would pray, you know the minister was happy to do that I don't know what went on with him and Phillip in terms of faith because I don't know, but I think there were quite a lot of in depth discussions but that's out of my sphere. It's that openness it's that willingness it's that not shying away from this horrible fact. And that was interesting there were some people who couldn't quite get to grips with the fact that Phillip was going to die and I'd got this fact quite clearly in my head and that I had to be quite clear to one or two people I don't think I was horrible and said, I don't think Phillip will be here at the end of the year and people couldn't quite believe that, so that was a bit tricky. And you know it's a hard thing to hear, isn't it?

May identifies three men who were just there for her. She knew that the minister would pray and she believes that he and Phillip spoke deeply about faith. She returns to the theme of openness and not shying away from the horror of death. She recalls there were some who could not understand that Phillip was going to die and May felt that she had to be clear to one or two about Phillip's impending death, something she recognises as hard to hear.

Int: Yes. Still being supported by those people?

May: Yes

Int: Find it easier to talk to women or men about Phillip's death?

May: You see am I talking about family or friends or colleagues?

Int: Everybody

May: I might put it another way if that's all right. I had a lot of sup-port from both males and females very positive. The only two negative, not negative, possibly inappropriate conversations were with men who thought they were doing their best but were completely off target.

The interviewer prompts with a question about talking gender and May responds by asking which particular group are being referred to. The interviewer responds with an inclusive everybody and May re-defines the question again. She begins by recognising very positive support from men and women but goes on to say that there were two negatives, then re-defines it as inappropriate, conversations that were with men, who, although they were doing their best, were completely off target

Int: In what way?

May: I knew you were going to say that. They both, wanted to talk about their own experiences and they both wanted to let me know that their experiences had been awful and they both wanted me to know that, it would make me a better person in the future because I would be able to draw on my experiences to support other people in the future. And I went off both of them.

In describing inappropriate conversations with men, May confidently generalises about what they 'both' wanted to talk about: experiences, awful experiences, being a better person and able to draw on experience in the future. And as May says, she went off both of them.

May: And I don't think Phillip would have ever done that, I don't they, he would have done that. No, I'm sure he wouldn't. But maybe what I had from them, cos I've talked about courage before haven't I, and that people would sort of in, well I haven't said in tune but people were in tune. Maybe that's because they weren't in tune and maybe that's because they were embarrassed. I'm using the word embarrassed in inverted commas because I can't think of another phrase, to be talking to me about it. But we were in circumstances such that they had to talk to me. So, they couldn't walk away and avoid me, they couldn't cross the street.

What May is saying here is that it takes courage to be 'in tune' with someone who is bereaved and that she is sure her late husband would have understood that they were 'embarrassed' in talking to May about Phillip's death, but it was unavoidable. It seems as if May feels that Phillip would not have criticised a couple of stumbling males for not having the resources to face her bereavement with courage.

May: But certainly, talking to women, is probably easier but then I'm a woman so. But you know I've spoken to the minister (male), I've spoken to both my brothers, I've spoken to my brother in law, colleagues. I have spoken to lots of men, but I suppose, but my immediate circle is more female based. But in terms of turning it round I would say the only two people who I felt weren't in tune were two men.

Here, May asserts that talking woman to woman is probably easier, although she then goes on to identify five or more men who she has been able to speak to, although her circle is more female based. By implication all of these people have had the courage to 'tune in' to her grief. It is just those two men who could not.

Int: Is there anything else you want to add about anything?

May: Well it defines you a lot, doesn't it? It defines you because you're in a state of grief which doesn't really go away, it defines you because you suddenly find yourself becoming this, this other handle which is widow. It defines you because you are no longer part of a couple. It defines you because, well you've got a great sense of loss, and you know, that you can't ever retrieve it, so there's nothing you can do to make it better cos it can't ever be made better because it is, it is absolute loss. But I was loved and

*cared for and still am so I'm very I know I'm very fortunate I know that,
I'm very blessed. And I think, on the whole, in my circumstances, I think
people made enormous allowances for me really. But it doesn't really stop,
does it? And I felt very much in the very early days that, you have no
choices there are no choices at all you have to get up, you have to get on
with today because you can guarantee that tomorrow's going to happen
too. And it's not because I'm brave because I'm not, but you just have to
keep plugging away at it.*

The interviewer asks our standard question for closing interviews. May responds by saying that bereavement defines a person; the defining characteristics of being bereaved, for her are: omnipresent grief, which although might not always be foregrounded is always there; suddenly finding yourself re-classified as a widow; one is no longer part of a couple; there is a great sense of irretrievable loss that as an absolute loss is beyond healing. Having begun this list, May then reflects on how fortunate she was and still is, to be loved and cared for and to have people making enormous allowances. May then returns to grief and reiterates that it does not really stop, and that despite this, individuals have no choice but to get up and get on with life. May does not see this as personal heroism, but as a simple necessity – 'you just have to keep plugging away at it'.

May: No more that's enough

Int: Absolutely fine, thank you.

*May: It's horrible isn't it, it's not good (chuckling) I wouldn't wish it on
anybody. But you, we know people are going to face it and people can't
see it and I, I've said so often that I don't want them to know but, one of
you is going to face it. But you know we can't live our lives waiting for a
partner to die. I mean we've got to live our lives living it with that person
or those people, how, you know whether it be family or single or whatever.
I was looking at pictures of, of my daughter today, as a little girl and you*

know it is another life that I led once but that would be the same whether Phillip was alive or not, it was another life when they were little, when she was a teenager, when she was a baby, you know they were just they are other lives, but, those lives have gone now and I'm leading a completely different life now. Was never written, that's why it was never planned

May then declares she has had enough; the interviewer thanks her, but then May goes on to continue her definition as 'horrible', 'not good', 'not to be wished on anybody'. She goes on to say that life changes and that she can see different spaces which she illustrates by reference to family photographs.

WHAT DOES MAY TELL US ABOUT BEREAVEMENT?

May is able to list what she sees as the characteristics of bereavement. First of all, omnipresent grief which is also permanent. Secondly the sudden definition as a widow, meaning you are no longer part of a couple. Thirdly a sense of irretrievable loss that is beyond healing and fourthly that grief is horrible yet has to be faced up to. It seems as if grief is another life which she illustrates by citing family photographs.

LONELINESS AND BEING ALONE:

May sees a difference between being lonely and being alone. She says that she is not lonely in her own company, but that she feels alone when she has no one to talk to about work-related incidents or personal reflections.

GENDER:

May initially re-defines the question several times and asks which particular group is being referenced. She then re-defines the question by turning it around to identify where conversations were inappropriate and refers to two men who were completely off target. In May's terms, it is as if they did not have the courage to 'tune in' to her and that she felt they were too 'embarrassed' to talk to her although conversation was unavoidable. May says that she finds women easier to talk to, but also adds that that is probably because she is a woman.

HONESTY AND COURAGE:

Because both May and Phillip knew that death was imminent, they both felt it was important to be honest with each other. This also required them to be honest with family members and with friends and acquaintances, which May admits needed a tremendous amount of courage. However, because they were so honest with everybody, they received a lot of support as a result.

FAITH AND SUPPORT FROM THE CHURCH:

For May, her faith is extremely important and that both she and Phillip felt their faith had been strengthened during his last few months. For May, her conversations about faith elide into conversations about support from the church. May says she never felt 'unsupported by her faith'. May refers to the support from church being 'tremendous' even though they had ceased to attend due to family life. She does however talk about the time she went to another church with the minister and his wife and that she found it 'very, very, very, very' good because they felt accepted as members there.

The support, however, from her previous church was very practical in dealing with funeral matters; but very compassionate otherwise.

Subsequently, May says she finds going to the Cathedral 'wonderful'

A CHRONOLOGY OF SUPPORT:

May's chronology begins before Phillip's death. May's starting point seems to be the support for Phillip in being able to talk with a minister about his impending death which ultimately strengthened both Phillip and May's faith.

She then goes on to talk about the love and care she received from her community. The funeral director was, May says, excellent. Her family, friends, colleagues and work places for both Phillip and May were also extremely supportive. Immediate colleagues were supportive and also the place of work in terms of cards and flowers and organic food boxes. In the last weeks of Phillip's life and in the subsequent weeks, a woman member of her church provided food on a regular basis for her. May found it very helpful to be treated 'normally' in such abnormal circumstances, for example when her neighbour called in to borrow some olive oil. She felt supported through knowing that others were grieving with her. As we mentioned earlier the support, love and care from the church members in participating in Phillip's funeral was also much appreciated. May refers as well to the continuing support from a local woman minister.

Everything May did, was either in relation to Phillip, a response to his death or a response to what May had to do because Phillip was not there.

13

HONOURING OTHER PEOPLE'S STORIES

THERE WERE SEVEN people generous enough to share their experiences of bereavement with us and, in sharing those experiences, we had not fully anticipated the emotional labour involved. It was a struggle for our informants who we were asking to re-live what was probably the saddest moment of their lives. To be able to talk about this so openly must have demanded considerable courage. That they were willing to re-live that time with us has been a privilege. We had not fully expected the demanding emotional work of actually conducting the interviews, nor had we thought that it would be so difficult to read through the transcripts afterwards. Finally, on this point, there were many occasions when analysing the data that we found ourselves on the verge of tears and being kind to ourselves, we interrupted the analysis. Those employed to do the transcriptions told us they also found the experience emotionally demanding and we are grateful to them for undertaking this task.

Kvale and Brinkmann (2009:130) advise researchers to "make the social context explicit during the interview, and also the emotional tone of the interaction, so that it is understandable to the readers." We trust that our remarks above indicate the emotional work of the interview, its transcription and its analysis. We have not previously seen the latter two stages of the process recognised as demanding emotional work. Neither have we seen the courage of those interviewed being recognised either. It may be that the focus of our studies draws on the sensitivities of others which may in turn lead us to recognise a greater range of emotional work and courage.

In our Introduction, we said that grief is likely to be a deeply personal experience and at the same time a special kind of social experience and we recognised that "one grief throws no light upon another". (Barnes 2013:69) Whilst it is therefore difficult for us to make generalisations, we can say that we found very little evidence of the five stages of grief Kubler Ross identified. None of the stages Kubler Ross identifies appear to be obvious in a respectful reading of our interview transcripts. One of our informants cautions us against trying to generalise about bereavement and grief saying that he thought 'bereavement was the same for everybody yet completely different for everybody'.

We made sense of each interview by reading them together, sometimes out loud and then co-writing first the commentary within the text and then a set of concluding remarks. During this process, we also included field notes where they helped us understand what we were being told. It can be seen that, apart from our common opening reflective question ("What does this story tell us about grief?"), no one summary shares a common set of headings with another, let alone common interpretations of the experience of losing a loved spouse.

We had thought that the semi-structured pattern of our interviews would lead to some potential comparisons in chronology but even that was very difficult. Several of our transcripts suggest that our informants' recollection of the time preceding the actual moment of death is very clear. Whenever an informant recollects the detail around the time of their spouse's dying they also recall the kindness of others even though in some cases there was a feeling of vagueness about what happened following the death.

We anticipated that our semi-structured interviews would lend themselves to the production of a kind of chronology of grief, distinct for each informant and yet likely to share some characteristics. Our analysis, however, did not allow us to identify much in the way of common themes. Perhaps this is hardly surprising, since we had no intention of producing some grand meta-narrative based on our seven interviews. Although grief was commonly recognised, it is characterised by very individual responses. We found that Amy, Ellie and Ian talked about grief; May talked about bereavement while throwing some light on grief; Barry offered us reflections on grief and Saul and Charlotte both talked about facing up to grief.

For Amy, grief is associated with practical activity. Amy acknowledges the support of her daughters in coping with the practicalities of bereavement. It is the women members of the hospital staff that are particularly recalled by Amy. So, when we go on to discuss gender, we will pick this theme up again.

Ellie had been bereaved for longer than the rest of our informants and so we found it particularly telling that she told us grief goes on, it never goes away and that there remains the hurt of knowing that she will never see her loved one again, nor will she be able to talk to him again. Ellie observed that some people assumed that once she had been bereaved for a year, the expectation was that she 'should be over it by now'. However, Ellie tells us that there is still that 'great big hole' in her life, although throughout our interview, and by her own assertion, her memories of her partner are mostly celebrated with good memories and laughter.

Ian, too, speaks of the huge 'hole' in life caused by the loss of a partner. He suggests that we are unprepared emotionally for such a loss and believes that caring for others helped alleviate and avoid pain.

Our informants tell us that bereavement and the associated grief has left a huge 'hole' in their lives, but even so, this is not always overlaid with sadness. Indeed, in time, it may even be possible to celebrate their lives with laughter.

A sense of embarrassment about bereavement and grief informs Barry's responses to us. Prior to his bereavement, he felt a sense of embarrassment when talking to those who were bereaved. He now recognises this in others and has developed strategies to put others at their ease when talking to him about bereavement. He tells us that he does not want his memories of his wife to be dulled or his feelings eroded. He sees grief as a 'little black cloud over one'. He cautioned us against trying to generalise about bereavement and grief and we have tried to keep this caution in mind.

May also speaks of people being 'embarrassed' because they were unable to be attuned to another's grief. She goes on to speak of bereavement as a form of definition and here May interleaves bereavement with grief and a great sense of loss; one that is impossible to make good because it is an absolute loss. She goes on to assert that all of us with partners know that one or the other will die first, but we cannot live our lives on that basis. We have to live our lives and face it.

Facing up to grief is a theme in Charlotte's and in Saul's narratives. They both speak of a 'struggle' with grief. They tell us of its devastating impact, of it being impossible to ignore or hide ("under the duvet") from grief. They both reject the idea of 'wallowing' in grief and believe we must all face up to it. It is a painful reality we have to learn to live with. Both reflect on their memories of someone with whom they had a special understanding, and Saul says that 'dwelling on the good memories of his relationship' was one of his coping strategies. We trust that this brief resume on the theme of grief illustrates the diverse range of responses our interview data picked up.

However, our immersion in the seven narratives provided by our informants, led us to think that perhaps a key underlying theme, albeit played out in different ways for each of our informants, was that of being lonely and being alone.

ON BEING LONELY AND ALONE:

Although not always a "headline", all of our informants speak, when prompted, of how they distinguish between being lonely and being alone, although the distinctions do not equate directly with each other. We can note that Amy speaks of being 'alone' when dealing with day to day household management; Barry problematises the implicit distinction between lonely and alone although he does speak of psyching himself up to go to cinema, concerts and so on, on his own. Saul, on the other hand, says that he is fortunate in living with his daughter, and this shelters him from being alone. He also emphasises that because of his belief and faith he is never 'lonely'. Charlotte told us that she 'needed to be on her own', but when she says this she means her and her two daughters, although when she refers to 'hiding under a duvet' it is her responsibilities for her children that bring her out of hiding. She, too, mentions household management responsibilities as does Ellie, however her son is able to take on those responsibilities. Ellie goes on to further elaborate, saying "you can be in a crowded room with loads of people and still feel alone. But if you've got something to keep your mind occupied you can still feel lonely. Feeling alone is the backbreaker because you feel as if there is nobody to help you, nobody there to rely on, to back you up if you're feeling down." Ellie's remarks resonate with Charlotte's comments, in that there is nobody there who is just the person there for you. Ian, on the other hand, says he does not feel unhappy in his own company but does admit to feeling vulnerable when anything goes wrong. May finds there is a big difference between being lonely and being alone and thinks that as a person she is "very content" in her own company, so does not feel particularly lonely. Being alone, for May, is all the decision making, dealing with big things or "tiny wee little tiny things that really upset you. It's the sort of alone that you need to talk something through, so I've been very fortunate" (here she is referring to visiting a friend in her pyjamas). In this context, we can note that all of our informants pay tribute to their children, often, but not always, mentioning a son or daughter who was particularly helpful.

MOSTLY MEN:

For Barry, it is going out on his own to events that were formerly "couply" for him, that makes him feel alone. So, for example, going to the cinema on his own was difficult without Pauline. For him, being on your own is social, that is inter-personal. He comments on 'always having so much to do around the house, to ensure he does not necessarily feel lonely, which is intra-personal. Although he does not speak of being 'lonely' we find his comments rather soulful. Initially, Barry wanted someone to go with to the cinema or theatre, but 'got over it', which required him 'psyching himself up to go on his own'. When Barry speaks of his positive experiences of the arts, after Pauline's death, they are generic, whilst miserable experiences seem to be specific.

In Saul's interview, the interviewer couples loneliness with being on one's own. So, Saul does not actually have to distinguish between the two. He sees a social side, which we have suggested covers 'lonely' where his daughter, friends and his dog are a comfort and a spiritual aspect to loneliness, where his faith shields him, whilst acknowledging the 'tremendous void' in his life, which we see as his understanding of Esther's death. It is a mixture of social and spiritual in which he sees himself as following his calling to serve God every day, and spiritual in recognising as he and Esther used to share, that 'we're in God's hands'. Saul's faith and his calling are inter-twined as both intra and inter-personal.

We had to look closely to see that Ian did distinguish between being lonely and being alone and although happy in his own company and not lonely, as such, he is very aware of being 'alone' when things go wrong. Ian speaks with some caution and, again, 'alone' seems to connect with practicalities whilst 'loneliness' has a much wider, usually social, meaning. For Ian, his responses are entirely at the inter-personal level.

Two of our male informants seem to offer a fairly narrow definition of 'alone'. Saul does not speak of it. All three offer a broad definition of 'loneliness'. Only two of our male informants refer to domestic practicalities. For Barry, they stop him from being lonely; for Ian they highlight the times when he is alone. Whilst all three speak of loneliness, its meaning varies. For Ian, it is essentially a social phenomenon, for Barry domestic practicalities mean that he rarely feels lonely. For Saul, being alone is not an issue, whilst loneliness has both practical and spiritual meanings.

MOSTLY WOMEN:
Amy is not lonely because she has 'plenty of friends', so there is company but you are still 'alone'. 'Alone' is difficult at 'couple events' and going out was a real effort and as Amy says if she didn't she "really **would** be on (her) own". Initially, Amy was dreading 'couple' events, but the kindness of others eased this for her and seemed to militate against Amy's sense of loneliness. Amy speaks of being busy and adopting tactics for widening her horizons and she speaks of the importance of others in helping her make her house **feel** more welcoming.

Although Amy deals with being 'alone' in some detail, we introduced the idea of kindness mitigating loneliness. Amy defines this aspect of grief as "it's not about being lonely....it's just that you are alone.." and then Amy speaks of domestic tasks. When Amy speaks of being alone it usually refers to practicalities and when she speaks of loneliness it appears to be a social product.

For Charlotte, being lonely is something she still finds very hard, four years after her husband's death. Sometimes, although she could have done with spending time with people, she did not want to be a 'burden' to anyone. Charlotte describes it as a feeling that 'comes and goes'. She says that anybody can be lonely, hence lonely, for Charlotte, is a social occurrence. Being alone is a separate state from being lonely. Being alone has two components: one is a time to grieve, reflect and cry if needed, the second is being 'without someone you were really close to being around'. It has much more to do with being a widow than being lonely.

Ellie, on the other hand, being alone is a 'back breaker', because there is no-one else to rely on or back you up and pick you up 'when you are down'. She adds that it 'can be nice to be alone', making time to think and time to cry, rather like Charlotte's experience. But, unlike Charlotte, being alone is social, knowing who your true friends are. She says that you can be lonely in a 'crowded room'. In the end, for Ellie, lonely is not social, whilst alone is both personal and social. Because of Ellie's interpretation, we saw her use of being 'alone' as a feature of her discourse.

May says that she is not lonely in her own company, but that she feels alone when she has no-one to reflect with; so being alone is personal and practical, whilst lonely is straightforwardly personal. She speaks of being alone in terms of decision making and needing to talk something through 'when you need to do so'.

Our four women informants provide interesting contrasts. For Amy loneliness seems to be social and is deflected by keeping busy, hence it is both intra-personal and inter-personal. This view chimes with Charlotte's response who adds to this her concern with the inter-personal, being a burden to others. Ellie, like Amy, sees loneliness as deflected by keeping busy. For her it is possible to be lonely in a crowded room, hence intra-personal. May positions loneliness as inter-personal and intra-personal by simply saying she is not lonely in her own company.

Being alone for Amy is a mixture of the social and the practical. For Charlotte and May, being alone is missing being able to have a conversation at a time it occurs in one's mind, an intra-personal concept.

ON NO LONGER BEING A 'COUPLE':
Not all our informants' remarks offered ready gender distinctions, for example, the issue of no longer being a couple seems to resonate for Barry, Ellie, Charlotte and Amy.

Whilst Barry anticipated that he could console himself through engaging with the arts, he found it hard to do so on his own. He speaks of going to the cinema on his own for the first time since he was eighteen. He tells us that he actually 'psyched' himself up for this. But having been to a couple of operas and several concerts, he says he has got over that: "That's fine now."

Amy gives us a fleeting commentary of the difficulties of being single when it comes to parties, weddings etc.

Charlotte used to feel comfortable going out for coffee or a drink with her male colleagues when Paul was alive, but since Paul's death has felt 'weird' at doing this, because she perceives that others may question her behaviour as a single woman.

She has become more cautious as part of safeguarding herself.

Ellie describes her situation at greater length. We note that at the time she was bereaved she was much younger than our other informants. In this context, it might not be so surprising that her friends felt obliged to make arrangements for Ellie to meet suitable "men". Of 'double dating', Ellie says: "You can have a laugh and a giggle ……… But they don't have to pair you up with somebody…….people do try and pair you up so that you're not lonely, sad, whatever." She goes on to observe that that was not how she actually felt, "just their thoughts."

Four out of our seven informants had some observation to make on having become single again. For Barry, it is no longer a problem; for Amy it is easily disposed of; for Charlotte and Ellie there is a sense of external expectations. For Charlotte retaining work based friendships with men is now 'weird' and she is careful to protect herself. Ellie saw the attempts of others to pair her up as their meeting their own concerns. She is rather reminiscent of Julian Barnes (2013: 107) when he says:

" some kindly want to solve you….as if that were obviously and necessarily the solution" (to his grief)

We have moved from considering our informants' views on being lonely and being alone towards the attempts of others to resolve these issues for them. In some ways, this might be seen as the end-stage of a chronology of grief, although when we return to our transcripts it is difficult to locate these feelings at a particular point in our seven individual narratives of grief.

CHRONOLOGIES OF GRIEF?

Every interview begins with either a question or an instruction. There are only tiny differences in the phrasing of this introduction to the interview. In essence, the interviewee is asked to talk through what happened after the death of their loved one, usually named, especially those people outside your family who helped. This remark is sometimes framed with the addition of "Who helped you most?" and sometimes as "During those difficult days…." Four out of seven of our respondents seemed to be reluctant to respond to the question. So, from our male respondents we get "I'm the wrong person to ask…"; "Well the first thing is that it was no surprise at all…"; and from May, an attempt to clarify the question whilst from Amy, she talks about events immediately prior to the death of her husband. Saul, Ellie and Charlotte attempt a straight answer. All of them then go on to talk about the support they received from various members of the family. Barry, Amy and Saul make immediate reference to their children and the support they provided. Ellie talks about the help she received from her sister and Charlotte talks about her mother's help. May talks first about the help her husband gave her prior to his death, and then goes on to answer the question. Firstly, she briefly acknowledges help from her family as a given, but then she goes on to talk about the help she received from the funeral director and her husband's work place.

Having developed an analysis of each of our informants' narratives, we can confidently say there is no single story of bereavement and grief.

We found a sense of sequence in Amy's narrative but this was not overt in her re-telling. She tells us that social interactions immediately after James' death were a blur to her. Barry provides a careful chronological ordering although he had to re-start several times to satisfy his own re-telling. He speaks of shock, surprise and protective feelings for his wife and is then vague about almost everything (e.g. funeral arrangements, neighbourly involvement, all a blur) immediately after her death. For Saul, his brief chronology begins with his sense of relief at the end of Esther's suffering. Charlotte provides a deeply personal chronology taking us through the changing phases of her feelings. Ellie has no real chronology but talks about keeping busy. Ian makes no attempt at a chronology. May's chronology begins with support before Phillip's death and the support of the community afterwards. Most of our informants valued others within their chronological re-telling. Specifically, these others are: family members; professional help, including a funeral director; community; local churches and a woman minister; friends and colleagues from work; and those who support without intrusion or being judgemental. Within their chronologies, May, Amy and Charlotte make reference to their spouses; one wanting to act in accordance with her husband's wishes; one keeping busy at times that were previously special to them, and one referencing the love and care they shared.

Not all of our informants made any reference to any aftermath in their chronologies. However, for Amy it was important when her house became a 'home' again and she acknowledges that grief still hits unexpectedly. Barry is very precise about the miserable outcomes of his attempts to engage with the wider world. Charlotte, following her pattern of mixing emotion and practicalities, speaks of preparations for a very special funeral service. She speaks of a long journey and three women who help her through this, also of medicalised grief, of extreme loneliness and of two women who helped her with these. May tells us that she appreciated food being provided, found it helpful to be treated 'normally' and supportive, knowing others were grieving with her.

INFORMANTS' IDIOSYNCRATIC TALK:
Some of our informants shared with us their unique speech 'mannerisms' when talking about their bereavement. We have noted the occasions on

which these mannerisms were used and on the basis of these occurrences we have suggested some possible meanings for these. For Amy it seems as if, in retrospect, she wants to step outside her pain at James' death by using the word 'daft' at the start of her recollection of events. The first time is a reflection on her own shock to the possibility of bereavement and the second time is recognising a coping strategy used by professionals. We have noted that Barry has used the word 'technical' to describe financial matters but there are two occasions when he strays from this usage: firstly, to describe his emotional well-being and secondly to gloss medical detail. He also uses the words 'and so on' to cover emotionally difficult areas or medical details. He uses it again to extend our awareness of the range of help he received. While it is dangerous to generalise, it seems to us that he was using these mannerisms to communicate areas where practical and emotional difficulties were intertwined. Saul uses repetitions during the interview often to create a space while searching for the exact word he wants, usually to express his appreciation for the help that others have given him and on occasion to acknowledge that we are in God's hands. Charlotte also uses repetition often to emphasise the sustenance she has received from others and on occasion to describe her own difficulties. She uses the word 'weird' often linked to a social context and having been part of a couple. Ellie uses irony on several occasions during her interview and to us it seemed at once rather rueful and to demonstrate that she does not take herself too seriously. Ian demonstrates a capacity to make light of some genuine insights. Quiet, male response and respect is at once valued and devalued. He also seems to us to offer an exceptionally strong rejection of religious ties. Interestingly we found in May's interview only one repetition which was her description when visiting another church of finding it 'very, very, very, very' good. May's repetition is one of appreciation. This distinguishes it from the other idiosyncrasies of speech we have identified.

We think of these as a kind of verbal dance around painful moments and ideas; whether it is Amy's congratulation of a medical professional while her husband is dying, Ian's recognition of the kindness of 'blokes' or Ellie's ironic comment that Nick is a typical man, never replying to her. We think these speech anomalies hide pain, grief and affection.

GENDER

We asked a fairly straightforward question about who they found easiest to talk to about their bereavement, men or women. Although the question was always pretty similar, the answers were very varied with references to the help they received from men and women also dotted through the transcripts.

Amy names twice as many women as men in her dialogue with us. She valued women's support and mentions a lack of experience or time from male visitors. Men, she tells us, avoided discussion of bereavement and lacked an appropriate vocabulary for encountering the grief of another, indeed one was completely tactless. Other men were able to sympathise and to offer kindness and compassion. So Amy did not employ a simple polarisation. Women, she felt, have a propensity to reaching out to the grieving which seems to pose a problem for some men.

Barry found it easier to talk to women, and felt they were more interesting and beneficial to talk to, being tolerant of discussion of medical detail. Women, according to Barry are more valuable members of humanity, and more openly empathetic than men. Men, he felt, tended to talk about politics and themselves.

Saul alludes to the caring role that women take although, he says, that because some men can be tender hearted, he is unlikely to differentiate between them. We note that throughout his interview he spoke of women in general and of men in particular. Both men and women members of his family are, he tells us, emotionally close and willing to share his emotional burdens.

During her interview, Charlotte named four women who really helped her. She goes on to speak of one woman and one male minister who were supportive. We have already noted the three women who helped her in her grief and the two women, one man and one couple who helped her afterwards. Reflecting on her bereavement during her College experience, she recalls a male tutor who was helpful and a female tutor who was "horrendous." She speaks of two fellow students, both women, with whom she prayed. She makes a specific reference to the powerful support she received from a woman bereavement counsellor.

There are two significant women who helped Ellie - her sister and her counsellor. Because her husband was in the services, she found it easy to talk to men and mentions in particular, one male colleague who wrote a testimonial about her husband to Ellie which she found helpful. We found it unusual that Ellie spoke of two male managers who would pop in and see her.

For Ian ordinary people who helped, seemed to be men. He says that "blokes" minimise what they say; what they do is more important. He was confident that the women he knew would provide emotional support if he felt the need for it.

May turned our question around and talked about where conversations were inappropriate. She told us that she recalled two men in particular, who did not have the courage to tune in to her grief and were too embarrassed to talk to her. She said women were easier to talk to but that, perhaps, this was because she is a woman.

THE KINDNESS OF OTHERS

FAMILY:
We asked all of our informants to talk their way through what happened after the death of their loved one and especially who, excluding family, helped them through those difficult days. All of our informants made reference to the help and support that their families gave them. Apart

from May, our informants did not appear to register our interest in the support received from those outside their family. In May's case she simply states that she cannot exclude the importance of her family at that time. We suggest that this can be attributed to a tacit familial understanding whereby the informant recognises that their family is also grieving, albeit differently from them, and thus, there is that unspoken empathy that enables family members to envelop the bereaved.

One act of kindness from the family is illustrated by Amy's daughter, Jo, who protected her from unwarranted intrusion immediately after James' death. Another form of kindness is that received by Saul from his daughter, Diana, with her stoicism or 'realism' as Saul chose to interpret. He also mentions his other daughter, Florence, and his son both of whom offer emotional proximity. Charlotte, on the other hand, mentions her sister-in-law who helped her enormously with organising the funeral. Ellie found her sister to be the 'backbone' of her support, together with her mother, whose husband had died a while ago. Her son helps through doing the jobs her husband would have done and also offers her emotional support particularly at the times of anniversaries. Ian mentions his daughter helping him and May talks about the support, love and care from her husband and children.

Friends, neighbours and acquaintances:
Amy makes special mention of those visitors who stayed for a short while, such as Diana, which she felt was just the right amount of time. She was especially appreciative of the people from the university who were very kind in sorting out a hotel for people who were originally going to stay with her and for those members of staff who transported her to the Cathedral for the degree ceremony for Lionel and who 'surrounded her' and nurtured her. She makes special mention of two neighbours who called around with cakes which they had made which she said was 'really sweet'. Amy also mentions Ayleen who rang her every week to check she was all right and who sorted out someone for her to be with at Ayleen's daughter's wedding so that she would not feel left out. Rebecca is also mentioned as her 'mainstay' who was both spiritual and

empathetic. The women in church were referred to as 'listening, watching and being there'. The bank people were mentioned twice – first of all when Amy went to visit them and ended up crying and secondly when she was on the phone to them and again ended up crying – as being so kind and helpful. Susan is also mentioned as someone who called around and was there when things were hard. It is this helpfulness, support and kindness which seems to have enabled Amy to cope with everyday life initially.

Barry makes reference to the bank people as being very helpful when he lost some money, which they were able to sort out for him so that he was not without any.

Saul is particularly appreciative of his neighbour who not only offered practical help such as walking the dog, but also allowed him to talk, weep or 'just sit' with them. He found it helpful to be reminded to remember his wife as she was, which gave him strength to cope with his grieving. The church people were mentioned as well. They not only visited but also prayed for him.

Charlotte mentions the kindness of those people who took it upon themselves to cook and bring food for her and her daughters. She also talks about the woman minister, Susannah, and Helen, who understood her emotionally and did not seek to 'fix' the problem. In particular, she says how helpful Babs, the bereavement group leader, was in helping her to feel she was not going mad and what she was going through was normal. Dave and Alice were also reported as being very kind as they came and cut her grass without being requested – they could see her need and responded to it kindly. Charlotte is very appreciative of a tutor on her course who 'listened'. She was equally very touched by some friends who took her out on day trips.

Ellie talks about the friends from her husband's work who visited and were not afraid to talk about his death, which she found comforting. Similarly, the two managers from her own workplace were mentioned as not being afraid to talk about death.

Ian recalls the kindness of the people in the pub who moved away so that he could buy a drink. He was struck by the way in which they did not need to say anything, but that their actions said it all. He was also touched by the number of people who attended the funeral tea.

May was touched by the number of friends who brought her food boxes and flowers and the empathy they showed her as she felt they, too, were grieving alongside her, feeling her sadness and loss. Her workplace, as well as her husband's, were also particularly kind and helpful. She talks about the minister's wife making her pasta. Four churchgoers and three others in her church were of exceptional support to her. May also refers to the heartfelt written messages to her as well as the telephone calls that people made and she thinks that these must have taken tremendous courage.

SUPPORT FROM PROFESSIONAL BEREAVEMENT WORKERS:

Funeral directors:
Amy, Ellie and May all refer to the support offered by funeral directors. In their professional capacity, funeral staff offer sympathy and professional support; guidance over funeral matters; listen to the bereaved people's requests and show dignity and respect for the deceased which in turn reassures the bereaved that their loved one is in 'safe hands'. In Ellie's case, she was very touched by the funeral director remembering her at her mother-in-law's funeral a year after her husband died, who gave her a 'hug'. Amy refers to the funeral directors as 'being very kind'. May talks about the funeral directors as being 'excellent'. Where funeral directors are mentioned by our informants, it is not simply for their professional excellence, although that is recognised, it is also for their common humanity towards the bereaved.

Counsellors:
Two of our informants, both women, told us they had been helped by counsellors. It is interesting to note that in both cases the counsellors were women.

With Charlotte, the break through from feeling she was going mad, was when the leader of the bereavement group she joined told her that what she was going through was 'normal' and that she was not going mad. The other counsellor Charlotte approached was one she initially thought may be able to help her daughter, Mo, but Mo refused to interact with a counsellor, so Charlotte accepted the counsellor's offer to help her and continued to meet up with her for a year. Charlotte felt that although both her counsellors were women, this was because women are more drawn to pastoral work and to ask how you are feeling.

Ellie's comments about counselling are interspersed through her interview and she makes three separate references to counselling. Initially she tells us that she did end up having counselling although she did not want it. The woman counsellor came for four sessions at the end of which Ellie tells us she could 'smile again'. She goes on to say that people have said that when she talks about her husband, she smiles a lot, because he was her 'soul mate'. A little later she returns to the theme of saying 'No', but after a return to work she went as a result of the topic arising in a meeting. She tells us it was one of the best things she could have done. The interviewer asked what made the difference and she replies that she felt 'listened' to and that she was not made to feel embarrassed if she cried. Ellie said she did not feel 'judged' in any way. As a result of this, Ellie says she would recommend counselling to anyone. Towards the end of the interview, Ellie again reiterates how helpful the counselling had been and that for her it was a landmark in her grieving.

Medical workers:

Although Amy was familiar with hospital procedures, she became acutely aware of the kindness of some of the staff. She mentions in particular the consultants who were trying to break the bad news to her gently and enabled her to wash James. She also mentions the nurse who was very well intentioned and who suggested to Amy and her daughters that they 'might like to hold James' hand' at the time of death. The ward clerk was also very kind in what she said after James had died and later on when Amy went back to visit the ward. Amy's hospital team colleagues were also mentioned: Sam giving her a 'bear hug' and Gillian coming up to anoint James. Amy mentions the Patient Affairs team as being kind too. Amy was also very appreciative of the transplant team who rang the day after James died and were in her words 'so kind'.

Barry's narrative implies that he too is very familiar with hospitals and their procedures. In the end he only makes specific reference to a male nurse who rang him to gently break the news Barry was expecting.

Ian is also familiar with the hospital context and related procedures and he identifies the palliative care team. He expresses special gratitude to this team as he appreciates they were able to do the more personal care that his wife needed, thereby enabling him to be able to spend time focussed on her and not the chores of her domestic care. He also talks about the child psychiatrist whom he felt was 'very wise'. Ian asked him about how he should care for his children when his first wife died, and was told that he should talk to them because talking also involves listening and if you are able to talk and someone listens you can often find your own solutions to problems.

Ellie was very appreciative of the family G.P., who rang her up after her husband's death and spent time with her talking through the Coroner's report so that she was clear about what had happened and also had time to ask any questions she may have had. The G.P. also checked on her well-being.

Ministers:
Amongst the seven people whom we interviewed, only one did not mention a minister. Amy was very impressed by the female minister who came around and supported her with cakes and kindness. However, she was not so impressed by the two male clergy who visited, feeling that they were not at ease in such an emotional situation. Barry mentions the woman minister as being a point of reference and as someone who had previously led a neighbour's funeral. Saul was helped pastorally by William, a male minister, who came and gave him and Esther communion at home. He also talks about the women priests, who came from two churches, and helped pastorally as well. He refers

to Joshua, another male priest, whom he used to meet whilst walking the dog, who asked after him and assured him that he and Esther were in his prayers, and that they were thinking about him.

Charlotte found both the woman minister, whom her husband had asked to take his funeral specifically, and Ron as being very helpful after the death of her husband. However, she also mentions that she felt very upset when on being unable to attend morning prayers, due to her grief, no-one rang or texted her to see if she was all right. However, she does refer to the time when the staff were supposed to be having an away day, and she says that she is unable to go because it was her husband's anniversary, that the team organised a memorial service for her instead of going on the away day, which she felt was very kind.

Ellie remarks that she found the Reverend who did her husband's funeral and subsequently her mother-in-law's funeral as being very nice. She also talks about him giving her a card with his phone number on it so that she could ring him should she feel the need.

May refers to a woman minister and a male minister as being of particular support. The male minister came around and prayed with her husband and took the time to have long in-depth conversations with him. The female minister was one whom May visited, when she was feeling very low, in her pyjamas and slippers.

It would appear that the bereaved people's experiences of ministers is very varied. Wherever *anybody* shows kindness and compassion, this is acknowledged by our informants. Our evidence suggests that it might be especially helpful if all clergy were to hone their empathetic listening skills.

FAITH:

Our informants all talked about faith albeit to a greater or lesser degree. Amy comments on how refreshed she felt after visiting her spiritual director whose outlook was both spiritual and empathetic and how she regards her still as one of her mainstays in her life. Barry refers to himself as non-Christian, rather like Andrew Motion, but then goes on to say that he finds the Anglican services 'splendid' and he 'enjoys the hymns and liturgy'.

Saul has a great faith and tells us that he thanks God every day for his life and regards his calling in life to be one of service to God every day. In his words, he says: "We're in God's hands and always have been," which means a lot to him. For Charlotte, who identifies herself as a Christian, she finds herself berating her husband for being in a place where there is no sorrow or pain whilst she is left behind on earth grieving for him. She is honest with people who tell her that because she has got her faith it must be easier for her, to which she responds that it 'doesn't work like that really.' Ian tells us he did take Christianity seriously when he was a child and was nearly confirmed in the Church of England, but in the end, was not as he felt he could not live up to the principles of the religion. Since being medically trained, however, he has stopped having any belief.

For Ellie, she says she prays every night for her husband's soul and for departed relatives, but not for herself. She went to church as a young person and says that the Reverend was really nice. She eventually got christened with her brother, but no longer goes to church. She says she does talk to God about her troubles and that her faith has helped her to get over her husband's death, and that her faith has also provided her with hope.

May's faith is very important to her. She has never felt unsupported by her faith and has never questioned it. She is a churchgoer, attending the Cathedral in her Diocese.

For our informants, some of them have a very strong faith which sustains them throughout, and is a pillar of strength for them, even if they do not belong to a church. Apart from Ian, nobody mentions losing their faith as a result of their bereavement.

Whilst there is no single narrative here, there are some significant messages. Nobody says that they feel angry with God for the loss of their loved one. We see the faith expressed here as taking a number of different forms; from the quiet sustenance of familiar liturgies, we move to faith as a constant, strengthening the believer, affording a listening God who will provide for them and for the souls of the deceased. We also recognise a more complex grasp of the workings of faith which although bringing greater understanding, may not necessarily bring greater comfort. There is a recognition that just because someone has faith, does not mean that they do not suffer as much as anyone else in the same situation. This deeper understanding of faith enables those who possess it to minister to others in a similar situation, in a way which can hold the great truths of their faith tradition and the pain of individual believers (based on contemporaneous field notes). We do not see this as 'grief work', a term first coined by Freud in 1917 and a concept utilised in a range of counselling and therapeutic processes (Stroebe and Schut 2010). We are not making any claims for any specific bereavement related grief work.

OUR THOUGHTS:

At this point in our analysis we are going to try and tease out some implications for researchers and for all of those involved in the business of grief. We have tried to be transparent in the way in which we have responded to the seven narratives of loss so generously shared with us. We have also tried to treat these responses with integrity and believe that one consequence of this is that we are able to find few, scarcely any, unifying themes. We can say that at the end of our formal interviews, and when invited to make further comment, six out of seven of our informants added particularly salient comments. This could be attributed to a sense of relaxation of completion of the formal interview. We thought we were pretty chatty all the way through our interviews, but clearly the opportunity to make further comment opened a new space for most of our informants. We included this invitation more or less for form's sake and were intrigued by the additional data we were able to gather. Some previous research has led us to think there might be perhaps five stages of grief and loss, or really strong evidence of oscillation between coping and being unable to cope. While there may be hints of the latter, we could not find any

evidence of the former. In fact, we could identify precious little conflu-
ence between the different streams of narrative recorded in our interviews.
What was undeniable in the interviews in their transcribing and in their
analysis, was a great sense of grief. At some point in the development of
our data, nearly every participant, transcribers and researchers included,
were moved to tears. Perhaps, like one of our informants, those involved
in the research were "easy criers". In some ways, this work is permeated
by grief, although there seem to be as many kinds of grief as there were
people talking about it

Our informants told us that, with one exception, it was women who were
best able to attune themselves to their inner life when they were in grief.
It also seemed that if any person lacked sensitivity and attunement, then it
would sadly be men. We believe this echoes the work of Christian women
through the ages. It was, of course, Mary Magdalene who, through her grief
for Christ, was blessed with the first revelation of his resurrection. She, unlike the disciples who had left once they discovered Christ's body had gone,
continued to stay at the tomb grieving. She knew that his body had gone, but
chose instead to remain there with her sadness, Mary had an understanding
that grief has its own momentum and her capacity to be absorbed by this enabled her to see beyond it. She sets a precedent for all Christians, but perhaps
especially for women. It is as Colin Murray Parkes (1998:173) writes the person who is the most helpful to the grieving is:

> …"not the one who expresses the most sympathy but the person who
> 'sticks around', quietly gets on with day-to-day household tasks and
> makes few demands upon the bereaved."

We have already acknowledged a history of compassion from Christian wom-
en (Chapter 1). In the twelfth century, we find this constancy accompanied by scholarship and compassion in the work and writings of Hildegard
of Bingen (1098-1179). This same compassion and understanding that grief
should not be rushed or compartmentalised can be seen in the work of Julian

of Norwich. It is as if she acknowledges that even grief has its own place when she tells us that "all manner of things shall be well" Christine de Pizan spoke of the care and compassion that women were able to offer Christian martyrs. St. Teresa of Avila seems to take the same perspective when she tells us that it is through human eyes that Christ looks with compassion on this world. While men may have played a significant part in medieval rituals of death, it seems to be women who extended both comfort and prayers to the bereaved.

More recently, Kelly (2008:61) emphasises the importance of sincerity where:

> "…a person feels genuinely cared for not so much because she has received expert psychological assistance, important thought that is, but rather because she has received the gift of self from her pastor or counsellor.."

In the preceding section, we said we were unable to find any single narrative of faith, but we also noted nobody said they felt angry with God for the loss of their loved one; some took sustenance from familiar liturgies; others found faith as a constant strengthening them as believers and providing a listening God caring for them and the souls of the departed. We also noted that a complex grasp of the workings of faith may bring a greater understanding but did not necessarily bring greater comfort. It does seem likely that those whose understanding of faith has been deepened in this way, may be well equipped to care for others in a similar situation.

While we are unable to find any consistently gendered accounts of the bereaveds' feelings of loneliness and being alone, all our informants seem to grasp at 'busyness' as a coping strategy. Although we are reluctant to enter into any grand narratives of gendered bereavement, we might tentatively suggest that women are able to acknowledge that they miss the domestic dialogues of mutually shared lives. Our tiny sample makes it impossible to produce any typically male versions of grief.

Although our semi-structured dialogic interviews had the potential to allow our informants to be explicit about their chronologies of grief, we found it impossible to generate anything other than uniquely individual accounts of grief and although we imagined each would have a chronology, this did not turn out to be the case. We found ourselves very close to the position of Sandra Bertman (in Berger S.A.2011:6) who suggests that:

"grieving is a complicated and continual dynamic, that may overlap, may be of varying and unpredictable duration, may occur in any order, may be present simultaneously and may disappear or reappear at random. Implicit in process theories is the understanding that grieving may occur intermittently."

We have already noted the emotional labour of interviewing, transcribing, analysing and being interviewed. We think that while all of these are hard work, it is probably hardest being interviewed and being asked to re-live the loss of a life partner. We were not surprised, therefore, to find idiosyncrasies in our informants' individual lexicons. We suggested that these were a kind of verbal dance around painful moments and ideas. We have already suggested that these speech anomalies hide pain, grief and affection.

After we had struggled with the analysis of individual transcripts and our inability to generate any 'grand narratives' of love and loss, we found that our analysis of our informants' responses led to an extended focus on the kindness of others. It was as if we threw a stone in the pond and a ripple resulted. Some of the waves we anticipated: family, friends, funeral directors, counsellors and medical workers. We were surprised by the reports of kindness from neighbours and acquaintances and the sensitivity of the people in shops and banks. We were surprised by a certain ambiguity about the extent of kindness shown by Anglican ministers. Perhaps we should not have been, after all there is a history of avoidance amongst some Anglican clergy, for example Ayres Ed. 2003:131, Jalland 1999:221 and Gaskell 2007:109.

We shall return to these thoughts and consider their implications for researchers, ministers and others after we have reviewed provision in England for the preparation of Anglicans for the ministry. Our review will have a specific focus on explicit commitments to training on supporting the bereaved.

14

AN EDUCATION ABOUT CARING FOR THE BEREAVED

I N THIS CHAPTER, we will be reporting on and reflecting on the provision made in a selected group of Colleges committed to training ordinands for the Church of England. It might be appropriate at this stage to remind readers that the most recent statistical data available (Statistics for Mission 2014 accessed 20.05.2016) suggests that the conduct of funerals in churches and crematoria by Anglican ministers which thereby involves them with contact with the bereaved, outnumbers the conduct of marriages and of baptisms. Given that a total of 145,000 funerals were conducted in 2014, compared with 46,000 marriages and 120,000 baptisms, then it seems that the most predictable pastoral duty that an Anglican priest might be asked to conduct would be that of a funeral. McCartney (2014) speaks of the need to balance curing and caring for an aging demographic. In a context of an aging population, and funerals being the most frequently requested Anglican provision, we thought it would be sensible to explore the offerings that English colleges provide for Anglican ordinands.

In order to do this, we examined the on-line information published by twenty- three English colleges recommended by the Church of England for the training of prospective priests and genuinely and readily publicly available. We acknowledge that there are other colleges committed to the training of ministers for Christian traditions other than the Anglican. In keeping with the rest of this book, we are focussing on those committed to the Anglican tradition. We looked specifically for any explicit reference they made to working with the dying, conducting funeral services and associated responsibilities, working with the bereaved and showing compassion for the grieving. We obtained supplementary information from one or two colleges.

A summary of the outcomes of our survey is presented in Appendix B below. Appendix B is based on the list of colleges in England recognised as theological training institutions by the Church of England. Full details can be found on www.churchofengland.org/recognisingtraininginstutionschurchofengland. We also checked whether there was a specific module in the course to assist ordinands in their work, and whether or not there was any direct experience of the role of other grief workers included in the programme.

We found that six out of the twenty-three colleges whose documentation was easily accessible on the internet in April 2016 made some explicit reference to working with the dying. Of this six, four made reference to conducting funerals; one other college that did not make reference to the dying, did make reference to conducting funerals. Of the original six, five also mention working with the bereaved. We note that College 1 advertised a specific module in the area. College 13 also advertised a specific module and was the only course to make some reference to engaging with compassion. The three Colleges that make explicit reference to working with the dying and the bereaved and conducting funerals are all validated by Durham University. Only one College makes reference to engaging with compassion.

We acknowledge that all twenty-three Colleges covered a substantial amount of material relevant to intending ordinands. However, death and dying and bereavement care were not seen as important enough to be foregrounded in the prospectuses or plans of sixteen of them. We also acknowledge that death and dying and bereavement care could well be covered in pastoral studies, but this information was not immediately available. It also has to be noted that there was not much reference to marriage or baptisms either.

We formed the opinion that there was considerable emphasis on visiting the sick but rather less emphasis on visiting the bereaved, although, of course, where it figured in the training there was reference to making funeral arrangements. It rather seems that while dying parishioners received help through the priests' visits, the bereaved seemed to be left floundering. Since priests and places of worship seem to be involved in more funerals than weddings, then it would appear to be essential that bereavement visiting and training for it is of the highest quality. This is the one occasion where the church can be seen and can also be judged – by those of all faiths and none. It is the one occasion where the church can really make a difference where good bereavement care experiences can resound around a community and where people, rather than shunning the church doors, might feel it is a place of welcome, of support and of comfort. We shall discuss this later in this chapter.

Bereavement provides one of those opportunities where the gifts of all church members might be used. We would suggest this is an occasion where we can comfortably dispense with hierarchy. Although we are aware that a priest is called to be a 'servant and shepherd' of the people in the parish, and to 'prepare the dying for their death' (ASB 1980:356), many would also expect that their priest would conduct the funeral service and to offer the bereaved comfort, support and compassion. Having said this, we also feel that the priest should facilitate the bereaved in taking comfort and support from their parish community, especially where there are people in the church community who have particular gifts in this field. Good bereavement visiting that shows kindness and compassion and God's love to those in distress, is something that our informants remembered. Saul, for example, recalls the support he had from the chaplains in the hospital where his wife died and from the ministers in his neighbouring parish. He also reflects that although he is now aware that the church is still there for him, he acknowledges that they do not come around quite so much. Charlotte said that some support, particularly the very 'practical support' which showed the quiet kindness of the church family, was really good. However, later on, she found that her continuing grief was no longer acknowledged in quite the same way and that it very much depended on the personalities of the people in question as to how she was treated. She was particularly supported by people who did not think that they could 'fix it' and for her that made a difference. It was the people whom she felt she could talk to, because they would listen and understand, without trying to make things better, that was so important.

Osmer (2008:35) building on 1Thes 5:11 (NRSV 1995) reminds us that:

"it is important to begin with this understanding of the priestly ministry of the entire congregation. Priestly listening is, first and foremost, an activity of the entire Christian community, not just its leaders. It reflects the nature of the congregation as a fellowship in which people listen to one another as a form of mutual support, care, and edification."

WHAT ATTRIBUTES DOES A BEREAVEMENT VISITOR NEED?

Ewan Kelly (2008: 142) delves further into this notion of kindness and compassion by citing a hospital chaplain's way of working with the bereaved:

….."it was the Church's representative's humanity, personhood and compassion that parents remembered, not just what was said or done." He was so warm, it wasn't just a job for him. It was the way he was……was actually, you could actually see he was kind of, he was really upset as well.."

Kelly advocates reading Neil Pembroke (The Art of Listening 2002 and Working Relationships 2004) who states that there are two essential gifts a "spiritual carer requires in order to sustain those in need." He says these are compassion and charm, but that the gifts of discernment (that is being aware of other people's needs) and "self-awareness" are needed when visiting the bereaved (Kelly 2008:143)

Compassion is more than just sympathy or empathy. It involves listening, caring, loving and "being there for that other person." This is not the time for a priest to talk about their own concerns, but it is a time for giving the bereaved space – space to talk, space to cry and space for silence. Kelly's description of charm is perhaps best summarised as "being yourself" and not trying to be something you are not. This is where our proposal of involving others in the church with these gifts of kindness and compassion and being themselves, can be acknowledged. Such charm is also about discernment which Kelly describes (2008:146) as being in tune with the bereaved and knowing what their needs are and how, as the bereavement visitor, a priest can best serve these needs. This is about showing God's love for the bereaved. We are suggesting that rather than relying on a priest or minister, who may not have a wealth of experience, the church should use people who have the skill of discernment, who have good self-awareness and who have experience of bereavement and the pitfalls that come with it. Through using those people who have had experience of bereavement, then faith can be seen through the deeds carried out, very much as James 2:14-26 (NRSV 1995) advocates. It is such bereavement visitors who, with kindness and compassion, enable the bereaved to sing and dance and laugh again. They are amongst those who not only spread the Gospel but are also living it.

Robin Greenwood (2003:41) talks about the "frequency with which the church sets itself up to be irrelevant and peripheral." He goes on to discuss the ways in which the "language, concepts and practices (of the church) are self-limiting" and that the "persistent rootedness in the doctrine of individualism, dominated by incipient clerical control of the Christian community" only leads to the alienation of the very people it wants to reach out to. He continues by posing the question of how effective leadership is and asks whether now is perhaps the time to start reviewing exactly what good leadership is. By learning how to involve the church in the community a good leader can have a dramatic effect in the locality. However, the leader needs to be able to delegate, to be wise enough to know his or her own strengths and weaknesses and to be able to seek out those who are able, in particular social contexts, to offer something far better than he or she can. Greenwood (2003:128) strongly advocates a partnership for "ministry for mission." This involves dispensing with many of the boundaries we currently have – those of adhering to a structured hierarchy, a church whose services mean little or nothing to society today – and here we are not referring to liturgy but to the services the church can offer the local community.

If we are to take Greenwood's ideas of partnership into the context of bereavement, then a church serving the community is likely to foster a team of co-workers who can provide some quite simple things: an affectionate and respectful funeral service; people who can listen and care, who can be there for the bereaved; people who can be themselves when visiting the bereaved and those who have experience of losing a loved one pertinent to the bereaved, and cakes!

A simple act of discerning the gifts of the people in the church, could help bring that church into its community by using people who have been bereaved themselves and are at a stage where they could be helpful to others. It would also provide a solid foundation of good pastoral care woven into the church community, so that should the priest leave, the care will continue. This is not solely about bereavement care for the church members, which ought to go without saying; it is also about reaching out to those in the community who have been bereaved and their families, offering them on-going support and comfort.

This might provide "space for women's experience and leadership in an effort to form new practices of gender identity, relationships, and roles. This is an expression of the church's commitment to the praxis of Christian freedom and love."

(Osmer 2008:158)

Funeral directors invariably telephone the minister/priest closest to the deceased's person's home. It is at this point that the minister/priest could telephone the bereaved family and ask if s/he could call around with a member from the church thereby setting up a link that could be sustained by the minister/priest, the church member and the church as a whole.

The funeral service is also an area where, rather than adhering to the standard service, such as the very helpful ones in the Church of England's Pastoral Services (2001) a tailor-made service could be created. Many priests now contact the bereaved to discuss details of the sort of service they would like. Such services often include poems, music, a family member singing and, of course, eulogies from friends of the family. Thus, it often does not resemble the standard funeral service. If the bereaved feel that their requests have been listened to and included, this can be seen as extending the pattern of good pastoral care as well as the affection in which the local church is held.

It is worth reflecting on who might most appropriately conduct a funeral. Being asked to take a funeral service is an honour and a mark of trust. The funeral service is seen as an acknowledgement that someone's life has ended; an acknowledgement of that person's life and all that he or she has done during it and usually an acknowledgement of the love and respect of all those surrounding him or her. As funerals are not a sacrament, then it is possible for someone other than the minister/priest to take the service. If, for example, a bereavement visitor has established a strong relationship with the bereaved, through kindness and compassion, then it might be desirable for that visitor to take the service, or at least have a major role in it. We are suggesting a visible continuity in the care of the bereaved. It is about visibly "being there" and that has to be a key to good bereavement care; being prepared to step in and also to step out. Hence, we are talking about caring relationships and shared companionship (Graham 2002:49) leading to what Graham calls "a focus on pastoral agency" (Graham. 2002:48). Our research confirms that such agency often lies in the gifts of women and can be, as Graham (2002) suggests, disavowed by an undue focus on the priestly role which tends to be masculine. The kind of continuity and care we are talking about relies on what Graham (2002:55) calls "the gathered community" and draws on definitive bodies of knowledge. As Graham (2002:139) says:

> "Models of Christian pastoral practice within liberation theology ground the normative principles for social transformation in a model of action and reflection upon experience and social context. The criteria for authentic practice – the values of liberation – are both the sources and the objects of pastoral practice."

Such practice when dealing with the emotional challenge of another's grief ought to resist the desire to "flee to safety" (Ward & Stein 1975:612) hoping to avoid the inconsistencies that interfere with our effectiveness as carers. Such facilitation and support are not easily learned and might usefully draw on the strengths of the community that ordinands serve. We have also spoken of the emotional labour of listening to stories of another's grief and hope that reading those stories can help develop what Ward & Stein (1975) call "an appropriate emotional style". We have seen something of the specific role of women in the Anglican community. We recognise that it includes and transcends cakes and casseroles. We think such gifts help channel respectful concern and an affectionate opening of doors to another person's grief, demonstrating emotional sensitivity and a capacity to hold another's pain.

Concluding remarks:

We began this chapter by observing that Anglican priests conduct more funerals than they do marriages or baptisms. About a quarter of those colleges recommended by the Church of England for training priests made any explicit reference to working with the dying and only one college made any explicit public link between bereavement and compassion. We have suggested that working with the bereaved is an opportunity to engage the gifts of all church members. We said good bereavement visiting demonstrates kindness and compassion. Our informants appreciated being heard without feeling they were being 'fixed'. Compassion, in our view, involves listening, caring, loving: it also requires charm, that is being attuned to the bereaved. We have said that the church community is able to reach out to its locality through shared priestly listening and beyond shared action, being seen to be there for members of the community in grief, resisting the desire to flee to safety and sharing the emotional work of listening to and caring for the bereaved. While caring for the bereaved might be a space readily occupied by women, a women's room, priestly listening asks for more than this gendered response.

While we acknowledge from our own and our informants' experiences that such priestly listening involves understanding the way others may be feeling or coping, we would suggest that those priests who have themselves had a personal and powerful loss and had the opportunity to reflect on it, may often be in a good position to offer priestly listening skills to others. In this way, others could be trained to listen, and understand that this listening will involve hard emotional labour for both the speaker and the listener and that if this is done well, they can share and bring Christ's compassion to the bereaved and fellow priests.

Appendix A

Interview Schedule

a) Brief introduction – reiteration that if anything is too emotional, that there will be time for pauses, or for continuing on another day. Also reiteration that there is access to a trained counsellor, should they require their services.

b) Assurance that although the interview is being recorded, their anonymity will be retained, and that the transcripts will be kept on a password protected computer, with the audio recordings being deleted.

c) Questions to be asked:

   (i) Introductory question: I know this may bring back many sad memories, but I wonder if you could talk your way through what happened after your wife/husband died, especially about those people outside your family who helped you most during those difficult days?

   (ii) Can you remember what those people who supported you most said or did that made that special difference? Was it empathy/sympathy enabling you to talk about your grief, or practical support perhaps? Are you still being supported by those people?

   (iii) Being bereaved can mean loneliness – were you helped in any way to be able to come to terms with being on your own? Are you still being helped?

(iv) I know your husband/wife had a 'religious' funeral – are you able to talk about the sort of support the church gave you/or didn't give you?

(v) Are you still being supported by those people?

(vi) Did you find it easier to talk to women or men about your wife/husband's death? Why was that?

(vii) Is there anything else you would like to add?

APPENDIX B

Colleges 1, 2, 13, 18, 19 and 21 all mention that they provide tuition on working with the dying

Colleges 1, 13, 16, 18, and 19 give guidance on conducting funerals

Colleges 1, 2 13, 18 and 21 mention about working with the bereaved

College 13 talks about engaging the bereaved with compassion

Colleges 1, 2, 13, 16, 18, 19 and 21 have a specific reference about bereavement and the dying in their prospectuses

Colleges 1 and 13 have a specific module in their course on death and bereavement

College 1 provides academic studies in grief and death

College 2 provides tuition on end of life issues

College 3 provides a seminar on supporting bereaved children

College 4 says that it has 'relevant academic staff'

College 13 makes specific reference to grave talk and offers on-going support

College 19 offers hospital placements

College 22 offers healthcare placement for M.A. students only.

Colleges 5, 6, 7, 8, 9, 10, 11, 12 14 15, 17, 20 and 23 do not mention anything about dealing with death, the dying or the bereaved.

BIBLIOGRAPHY

BOOKS:

Alternative Service Book **(1980):** London: Hodder & Stoughton

Aubrey J. (ed Britten T 1881) *Remaines of Gentilisme and Judaisme* London: Leopold Classic Library

Ashcroft, M.E. (2000) *Spirited Women* Oxford: Bible Reading Fellowship

Ayres, J. (ed) (2003) *Paupers and Pig Killers* Stroud: Sutton Publishing Ltd.

Backhouse H & Pipe R (eds) (1987) *Revalations of Divine Love* London: Hodder & Stoughton

Barnes J (2013) *Levels of Life* London: Jonathan Cape

Bennett, A. (1983) *The Old Wives' Tale* London: Penguin

Berger P. L (1970) *Rumour of Angels: Modern Society and the Rediscovery of the Supernatural* London: Penguin

Bingen, H of (transated by Atherton M 2001) *Selected Writings* London: Penguin

Common Worship: Pastoral Services **(2000)** London: Church House Publishing

Davies J.J., Garner P., Lee J (1998) *Managing Special Needs in Mainstream Schools* London: David Fulton

Everly G.S. Jnr. & Lating J.M. (2012) *A Clinical Guide to the Treatment of the Human Stress Response* New York: Springer

Fairclough N (2003) *Analysing Discourse* London: Routledge

Gaskell E. (2007) *The Cranford Chronicles* London: Vintage Books

Graham E (2002) *Transforming Practice* Eugene, Oregon: Wipf & Stock Pubs

Greenwood R (2003) *Transforming Church* London: SPCK

Greer G. (1981) *The Obstacle Race: The fortunes of women painters and their work* London: Picador

Grey M (1993) *The Wisdom of Fools?* London: SPCK

***Holy Bible NIV* (1984)** Grand Rapids, Michigan: Zondervan

***Holy Bible NRSV* (1995)** Oxford: OUP

Houlbrooke R (2000) *Death, religion and family in England 1480-1750* Oxford: Oxford University Press

Jalland P (1999) *Death in the Victorian Family* Oxford: OUP

Kelly E. (2008) *Meaningful Funerals* London: Continuum

Kramarae C & Spender D (2000) *Routledge International Encyclopedia of Women* New York: Routledge

Kubler-Ross E (1969) *On death and dying* New York: Springer

Kvale S & Brinkmann S (2009) *Interviews – Learning the craft of qualitative research interviewing* London: Sage Pubs Ltd

Lamm M (2000) *The Jewish Way in Death and Mourning* New York: Jonathan David Pubs. Inc.

MacCulloch D. (2009) *A History of Christianity* London: Penguin

McCartney M (2014) *Living with Dying: Finding care and compassion at the end of life* London: Pinter & Martin Ltd.

Murray Parkes C. (1998) *Bereavement: Studies of Grief in Adult Life (3rd ed)* Madison:International Universities Press Inc.

Nodding N (2003) *A feminine approach to ethics and moral education* Berkeley: University of California Press

Osmer R. (2008) *Practical Theology* Grand Rapids, Michigan W.B. Eerdmans Pub Co.

Pizan, C de (translated by Brown-Grant R 1999) *The Book of the City of the Ladies* London: Penguin

Pollard A. (ed) (1987) *Children and their Primary Schools* London: Falmer Press

Schaused M (2006) *Women and Gender in Medieval Europe* New York: Routledge

Schillace B. (2015) *Death's Summer Coat* London: Elliot & Thompson Ltc.

Smith A (1759 reprinted 2006) *The Theory of Moral Sentiments* Mineola, New York: Dover Publications Inc.

Stroebe M.S., Stroebe W., Harisson R.O (eds) (1999) *Handbook of Bereavement: Theory, Research and Intervention* Cambridge: CUP

Swinton J & Mowat H (2006) *Practical Theology and Qualitative Research* London: SCM Press

Walter T (1999) *On bereavement: The Culture of Grief* Buckingham: Open University Press

Wengraf T. (2001) *Qualitative Research Interviewing* London: Sage Publications

JOURNALS:

Butcher H. & Eke R. (2013) *Forgetting kindness:politics, policies and practices in early childhood* in He Kupu Vol 3.2 pps 30-42

Eke R, Lee J, & Clough N. (2005) *Whole class interactive teaching and learning in religious education: transcripts from four primary classrooms* in British Journal of Religious Education Vol 27:2 pps 159-172

Fiddes P.S. (2015) *Acceptance and Resistance in a Theology of Death* in Modern Believing Vol. 56:2 pps 223-236

Fraser N. & Nicholson L. (1988) *Social criticism without philosophy: an encounter between feminism and post-modernism* in Theory, Culture and Society Vol 5:2 pps 373-394

Guest G et al (2006) *How many interviews are enough?* In Field Methods: Sage Journals Vol 18:1 pps 59-82

Gundel H. et al (2003) *Functional Neuroanatomy of Grief* In American Journal of Psychiatry Vol 40:11 pps 1946-1953

Holmes T.H. and Rahe R.H. (1967) *The Social Readjustment rating scale* in Journal of Psychosomatic research Vol 11:2 pps 213-221

Lyttle C.P. (2002) *Bereavement visitng: older people's and nurses' experiences* in British journal of community nursing Vol 6:12 pps 629-635

Paul K. (2015) *The Ars Moriendi: A Practical Approach to Dying Well* in Modern Believing Vol 56:2 pps 209-222

Roche E (1979) *The widow, her children and their worlds* in Barnado's Social Work Papers No: 7

Stroebe M & Schut H. (2010) *The Dual Process Model of coping with bereavement: A decade on* in Journal of Death and Dying (Omega): Sage Journals Vol 61:4 pps 273-289

Ward N.G. & Stein L. (1975) *Reducing emotional distance: a new method to teach interviewing skills* in Journal of Medical Education Vol 50:6 pps 605-614

NEWSPAPERS:

Brooks-Dutton B (2014) *"It's just the two of us now"* in *The Guardian Family* 03.05.2014 pps 1-2

Personal e-mail:

Stroebe M. (M.S.Stroebe@uu.nl) Subject: *Request for guidance* e-mail to V. Lee (vronlee@hotmail.com)

WEB SOURCES:

Archbishops' Council: Ministry Division *Four funerals and a wedding: a review of the legislation for parochial fees* www.churchofengland.org/media/56817   accessed 24.10.2014

Baker S.E. & Edward R. (2012) *How many qualitative interviews is enough? National Centre for Research Methods Review Paper.* www.eprints.ncrm.ac.uk/2273   accessed 09.10.2015

Berger S.A. (2011) *The Five Ways we Grieve – National Association of Social Workers pdf* www.naswma.org accessed 20.05.2016

Church of England *Recognised theological training institutions by the Church of England* www.churchofengland.org accessed 22.04.2016 and 29.04.2016.

Church of England *Statistics for Mission 2013* www.churchofengland.org accessed 24.10.2014

Church of England *Statistics for Mission 2014* www.churchofengland.org accessed 20.05.2016

Coffey J *Secularisation: is it inevitable?* www.jubilee-centre.org   accessed 24.10.2014

Cruse Bereavement Care *Feelings when someone dies* www.cruse.org.uk accessed 01.11.2014

Daily Mail on line *50 Best places to live in the U.K.* www.dailymail.co.uk/property/article_3364043 accessed 17.09.2016

Department of Health (2008) *End of life care strategy* www.dh.gov.uk/ publications accessed 09.09.2016

Grahn J (1982) *The work of a common woman – cited in Bereavement Booklet for Jewish Women 2002* www.jwn.org.uk accessed 02.01.2012

Graves D. *Julian of Norwich "In content: All shall be well –Article 31* www. christianhistoryinstitute.org accessed 17.10.2014

Gray T (1751) *Elegy written in a country churchyard* www.thomasgray.org.uk accessed 17.10.2014

Hanson R. *The Neurology of Grieving (Grief Recovery:implications of neuroscience and contemplative wisdom Slides 15 & 18 in Kara Slides pdf* www.wisebrain.org accessed 17.05.2015

Herald on line (Scotland) *Glasgow has lowest life expectancy for men and women in Scotland, figures reveal* www.herald.scotland.com/news/13184969 accessed 17.09.2016.

Herstoria (23.06.2012) *Suffragists and Suffragettes* www.herstoria.com accessed 26.09.2016

Higginbotham P. *The New Poor Law of 1834* www.workhouses.org.uk accessed 12.01.2015

Historic U.K. *The Spanish 'flu pandemic of 1918* www.historic-uk.com accessed 24.10.2014.

Holmes T. & Rahe R. (1967) *The Holmes and Rahe Stress Scale* www.jbc.ca accessed 17.05.2015

Jewish Women's Network (JWN) (2002) *Bereavement Booklet for Jewish Women* www.jwn.org.uk accessed 02.01.2012

Kiefer J.E. (1999) *Bibliographical sketches of memorable Christians of the Past – Hildegard of Bingen Visionary 1078-1179* www.justus.anglican.org accessed 17.10.2014

Living Heritage *Key Dates 1689 to 1829* www.parliament.uk accessed 01.11.2014

Macmillan Cancer *Bereavement information and support* www.macmillan.org.uk accessed 01.11.2014

Marie Curie *Bereavement information for family and friends* www.mariecurie.org.uk accessed 01.11.2014

Murray C (2003) *Grief, Loss and bereavement* www.encyclopedia.com accessed 24.04.2015

Poor Relief Act (1662) *The Poor Relief Act (The Settlement Act)* www.workhouses.org.uk accessed 01.11.2014

Prochaska F *The Church of England and the Collapse of Christian Charity* www.socialaffairsunit.org.uk accessed 24.10.2014

Regency Redingote (2012) *The Regency Way of Death: Furnishing the Funeral* www.regencyredingote.wordpress.com accessed 17.10.2014

Ruiz Romero M.I. *The Ritual of the early modern death 1550-1650 Universidad de Malaga* www.anmal.uma.es/numero17/Romerohtml accessed 17.10.2014

Smith A (1759) *The Theory of Moral Sentiments Chapter IV* www.marxists.org accessed 17.10.2014

Teresa of Avila quotes *(Author of Interior Castle)* www.goodreads.com/ authorquotes accessed 17.10.2014

Westminster Abbey *Unknown Warrior* www.westminsterabbey.org accessed 24.10.2014

Woodbury S. (2014) *Life Expectancy in the Middle Ages* www.sarahwoodbury. com/lifeexpectancyinthemiddleages accessed 17.10.2014

22580736R00147

Printed in Great Britain
by Amazon